ADOLFO KAMINSKY
A FORGER'S LIFE

Sarah Kaminsky

ADOLFO KAMINSKY
A FORGER'S LIFE

Photographs by Adolfo Kaminsky

Translated by Mike Mitchell

DoppelHouse Press • Los Angeles

Adolfo Kaminsky, A Forger's Life

BY Sarah Kaminsky
PHOTOGRAPHS © Adolfo Kaminsky
TRANSLATED BY Mike Mitchell

DoppelHouse Press © 2016

Adolfo Kaminsky, une vie de faussaire by Sarah Kaminsky © Calmann-Lévy, 2009

Cet ouvrage a bénéficié du soutien des Programmes d'aide à la publication de l'Institut Français.

This work, published as part of a program of aid for publication, received support from the Institut Français.

DESIGNED BY Curt Carpenter
PRINTED IN THE UNITED STATES

Publisher's Cataloging-in-Publication data
NAMES: Kaminsky, Sarah, 1979-, author. | Kaminsky, Adolfo, 1925-, photographer.
Mitchell, Mike (Translator).
TITLE: Adolfo Kaminsky, A Forger's Life/by Sarah Kaminsky ; photographs by Adolfo Kaminsky; translation by Mike Mitchell.
DESCRIPTION: Los Angeles, CA: DoppelHouse Press, 2016.
IDENTIFIERS: ISBN 978-0-9970034-0-6 (Hardcover) | 978-0-9970034-7-5 (pbk.)
978-0-9970034-4-4 (ebook) | LCCN 2016947348.
SUBJECTS: LCSH Kaminsky, Adolfo, 1925- | Forgers---France--History. | World War, 1939-1945--Underground movements. | Forgery--History. | World War, 1939-1945--Jewish resistance--France. | Palestine--Emigration and immigration--History--20th century. | Algeria--History--Revolution, 1954-1962.
BISAC BIOGRAPHY & AUTOBIOGRAPHY / Historical.
CLASSIFICATION: LCC D802.F8 K36 2016 | DDC 940.53/44--dc23

DoppelHouse Press
LOS ANGELES, CALIFORNIA

For Leïla

Preface

WHEN I WAS LITTLE I knew nothing about the story of my father's life. I was the youngest of three children. As far as I could see, I had a father like everyone else's, who always taught me to obey the law. At home he never talked about his earlier life, when he'd been a forger. There was one episode, however, that should have made me think. One day I got a poor grade at school. I was absolutely determined to conceal it from my parents. I decided to forge my mother's signature; I'd never have dared to try and copy my father's, it's absolutely impossible to forge. I practiced for a long time on draft paper before setting about it carefully. Later on my mother happened to come across my notebook and immediately realized that the signature was forged. I really got yelled at. Ashamed of myself, I took refuge in my bed. When my father arrived home from work, he came to my bedroom. Expecting the worst, to be hauled over the coals as never before, I hid under the blankets. He sat down on the side of the bed, my notebook in his hand, and simply burst out laughing. He laughed so much he couldn't stop. Puzzled, I poked my head out of the sheets. Looking at me with a big smile on his face, he declared, "But at least you could have made it a better one, Sarah. Look at this signature, how tiny it is!" Then he went away, laughing uproariously.

I couldn't say precisely when I knew. There was never a family gathering at which our father announced, "Children I have something important to tell you." It just happened as time passed. When I was very young, I liked to keep my ears pricked to hear what the grown-ups were talking about. I heard it said that he'd been in the Second World War, the Algerian War. But to my little girl's mind, 'being in the war' meant to be a soldier. I found it difficult to imagine my father, a pacifist and non-violent, with a helmet and rifle. Later on, books were published in which his name was mentioned; then there were documentaries in which he agreed to speak. Eventually, once I was grown-up, I naively thought I knew more or less everything there was to know. I couldn't imagine it would take me several years to gather together and compile all the elements of his biography. There were so many memories to be called up, people to be found, places to be visited.

A lot of travel was needed to find my father's former comrades. The ones I wanted to question were scattered all over the world. One was in Portugal, another in Algeria, yet others in Israel, in Switzerland, in Italy, in the United States, in Latin America... Some were missing, already deceased. It was a matter of urgency to collect as many accounts as possible before there were no more witnesses left. I realized that time had suddenly started to fly. My father was no longer young; he was about to celebrate his seventy-eighth birthday. I was twenty-four, and I'd just had my son, Alec. All this triggered something in my mind: for the first time I realized my father wasn't immortal. The birth of Alec brought its share of joy and wonder, but also this fear: was Alec going to have the time to get to know his grandfather?

If that didn't happen, would it be up to me to tell him the story of that remarkable life?

Alec was babbling away in his stroller when I walked to my father's to ask him if he would like me to write the book. He gave his approval immediately. When I was back home, he called me. There was one question bothering him. "Sarah, do you know if there's a statute of limitation?" It was the first thing he wanted to know: did he still risk going to prison, despite the thousands of lives he'd saved? For every time he'd gone to the aid of an oppressed people, he had been breaking the law. At best he risked being sent to prison for his commitment to these causes, at worst condemned to death, and that explains why it took so many years for him to agree to reveal his secrets.

We arranged to see each other every Tuesday and Thursday afternoon. I warned him, "You'll have to answer all my questions, even those that will take you back to past events that are painful. Are you really sure you want to share all that with me?" He agreed enthusiastically. However, the first session turned out to be a disaster. Concerned not to lose the least detail of our conversation, I'd brought a Dictaphone. As soon as I turned it on, my father's voice was transformed. It became hesitant, too low, almost inaudible. He answered my questions with stock replies or a simple "Yes," "No," "It wasn't quite like that," or mere grunts. At the end of the day I had no usable information. I told myself we'd never get there. At the next session I decided not to turn on the Dictaphone. And, as if by magic, it loosened his tongue, his normal voice returned. I realized that the Dictaphone, that simple, inoffensive mike, unwittingly suggested to him the idea of a police interrogation. As if in his eyes I'd become a Gestapo officer. Putting technology to one side, I went out and bought some school notebooks, in which I would record our conversations during a whole year of interviews. Little by little our relationship changed from father and daughter to that of confidants.

What struck me most in the course of our discussions was his feeling of being responsible for the lives of others and guilt at having survived. They are feelings he has retained throughout his life and which doubtless explains why he continued to forge papers for thirty long years, at the cost of all sorts of sacrifices. For sacrifices there were, and many of them. Financial sacrifices for, in order not to be a 'mercenary', he always refused payment for his forged papers, with the result that he was always broke; sacrifices in his relationships, for his double life caused many break-ups—his repeated unexplained absences made his partners think he wasn't truly involved or was even being unfaithful, and eventually left him; family sacrifices, since long before he married my mother, Leïla, he had two grown-up children by an earlier marriage... I was very little and had just arrived in France when my father introduced me to my half-sister and half-brother. Unfortunately he hadn't been able to bring up these earlier children, who were thirty years older than me, the way he would have liked. My sister told me that he once disappeared for two years without sending any news, nor even saying goodbye. They often thought he was dead, sometimes that they'd been abandoned. They had no idea that his long silence was aimed at protecting them. Now I could better understand why my father didn't really like talking about the past. And I realized how fortunate I had been to have a dad, a dad who was there.

The book, the culmination of many years of work, came out in France in 2009. In the meantime I had returned to my work as an actress and scriptwriter. My father and I were happy and excited to see the book published, yet we were gradually overcome with a feeling of melancholy. For us, moving on from such a marvelous venture was like having to say goodbye. It was painful. We had become accustomed to our little rituals, had shared our secrets over the past few years... And what was going to happen now?

I didn't know then, but a new story was about to begin, a story as rich and beautiful as the previous one. The book had a tremendous reception, which took us by surprise. It sold very quickly in the bookstores, and we were very much in demand with the press. There were laudatory portraits in the national and regional media, appearances on television and radio, reports on the TV news. I was asked to give a video-recorded talk on TEDxParis, which also contributed to the great buzz the book created. There followed one translation into a foreign language after another: Italian, German, Spanish, Hebrew, Arabic, Turkish and now English. We traveled around all those countries, met readers, booksellers, journalists. We haven't stopped spending time together, precious time, and the adventure of the book continues to this day. We regularly go to schools and colleges, where my father speaks. That's what he prefers above all: passing on his knowledge. The first time he addressed a hundred or so pupils of sixteen to seventeen, he was very moved by their empathy and attention at an age when people are often unruly. You could have heard a pin drop in the hall. They were completely absorbed in the story he was telling them, asking astonishingly pertinent questions. On the way home my father said, "Did you see how attentive they were? I'd never have thought young kids could be interested in an old dinosaur like me." I pointed out to him that those 'kids' were exactly the same age as he'd been when he joined the Resistance, which made it all the more easy for them to identify with him.

During book signings and meetings with readers quite a few people came along with old forged papers that had belonged to their parents or grandparents to see if, by chance, they happened to have been made by my father. These people confided in us, hoping to discover some chapters of their own family history through ours. We listened to so many stories, met so many remarkable people, that there would be no point in even trying to go into them all here. Among the questions I was repeatedly asked, I have chosen one directly concerning the process of writing which I would like to answer here: Why is the book written in the first person, as if my father were relating his own story, while I wrote it myself? In fact I started the manuscript in the third person and in the past tense. But, after having developed several chapters, I got stuck in the narrative, incapable of continuing. It wasn't the well-known 'writer's block,' since I knew exactly what I wanted to write. I was paralyzed. For months on end, with no idea why, the very thought of sitting down at my computer made me feel ill. I decided to take a break and devote myself to other activities. The weeks passed, and I still couldn't find a solution to my problem; I was starting to have serious doubts about my ability to complete the project. That is, until the day I realized that talking about my father in the past tense was as good as writing his obituary in advance. So while he was there in front of me, very much alive, replying to my questions, I had the feeling I was pushing him into his grave. I had a revelation: I had to let him speak! I deleted all my work and started from the beginning again, using the first person, giving him a voice.

On October 1, 2015 my father turned ninety. His life today,

together with my mother, is a world away from the torments he suffered during his years underground. He's happy to be a husband, a father and a grandfather. And particularly active for his age... For since the publication of the book he's started out on a new career. I've already mentioned the personal sacrifices he had to make. There is one that I've omitted. Refusing payment from the resistance networks that he served throughout his life, he made his living as a photographer in various fields: postcards, advertising photos, but also photo reportage on industry (the coal mines of the North, the French sugar refineries...). He took numerous photographs of works of art for exhibition catalogues and posters as well. And he was the regular photographer for the painters who were the precursors of kinetic art such as Antonio Asis, Jésus Soto, Carmelo Ardenquin, Yacov Agam... As a specialist for giant-format photography he produced photos for film sets for Trauner, the designer for Marcel Carné, René Clair...

Alongside this work he continued to take, for his own satisfaction, thousands of artistic photographs in the hope of exhibiting them one day. He developed the rolls of film and stored them in shoe boxes that he piled up on top of each other, without ever printing out the photos, because he had neither the time nor the financial means, so that no one has ever seen his work. Thousands of negatives hidden in boxes, what a waste! There are irreparable sacrifices, but this was not one of them, and it was perhaps not too late to start out on a career as a young photographer, even though he was over eighty. He finally decided to print his photos and unveil his artistic work with, as his favorite subject, a view of the world in chiaroscuro where the protagonists are workers, secret lovers, dealers in secondhand goods, real or pretend models, dislocated dolls, bearded hobos... From the flea market of

Saint-Ouen to the neon lights of Pigalle he has captured the looks, the solitary silhouettes, the lights, the elegance and the fringes, everything that goes to make up his universe. With the support of friends we have arranged several exhibitions at cultural organizations and Parisian galleries. His unpublished photos have had a great success. It was extremely moving to see him talking about his photos with other photographers, recognized by his equals (of which he was the doyen, of course).

Today my son is twelve. When I was his age, while my friends' dads were reading them Grimm's fairy tales to get them to sleep, my father was telling me stories about very ordinary heroes. These unassuming heroes had such a strong belief in their ideals that they managed to realize them when it seemed impossible. These heroes had no army behind them. In general they were just a handful of men and women of conviction and courage. At the time I didn't know that it was his own story my father was telling me. I did, however, understand what he was trying to pass on to me through these part-metaphorical, part-biographical 'stories'. They are the stories that I tell my son today to help him always believe in his dreams.

—Sarah Kaminsky
OCTOBER 2015

Prologue

"SINCE YOU WANT TO KNOW everything, tell me what you think you know about my life. For example, when did you learn that I was in the Resistance?"

"To be honest, I don't know. Even less about you being a forger. If we'd stayed in Algeria I might never have known about the Second World War. For me you were the Mujahid, *as they say."*

"But afterwards, in France, you knew?"

"Not right away. You didn't talk to us about it. I grew up thinking I was the daughter of a social caseworker who helped rehabilitate young delinquents, found work for them, taught them photography. But by keeping my ears open when the grown-ups were talking I got some hints, in bits and pieces. There were contradictions in what I learned—everything was confused. It was through a series of external events that I came to understand. There was that article in Minute, *the extreme right-wing weekly. You remember?"*

"Of course, I've even kept it. There, look."

"'The ex-forger rebuilding his life on moral principles. Today a former forger is keeping young people on the straight and narrow. This ex-member of the Jeanson network, who supported the

Algerian FLN against the French, has now taken on the task of helping our delinquents from North Africa get back into society...' Well, well!"

"After this article appeared, some of the young people I was dealing with made jokes—in pretty poor taste, I have to say: 'I have a cousin who needs some papers,' or: 'I happen to need several thousand francs.' "

"I remember much later, when you were putting the file of material for our request for French citizenship together, I saw some letters. There was one that aroused my interest. It was an expression of gratitude for your work for the French Army intelligence and counter-intelligence services in 1945. I said to myself, 'Wow, my father a secret agent!' Depending on people's point of view I heard you called a forger, a Resistance hero, a traitor, a secret agent, an outlaw, a mujahid..."

"And what did you think of all that?"

"That one day I'd have to clear it up. Look, I've made a list of people I'd like to ask about you."

"Let me have a look... Hey, it's a long list you've got there. Your work's going to be complicated. They're almost all dead."

When we'd finished scoring out the names of all those I couldn't interview, my list had been reduced by half and my father said, "That'll mean less work for you," making a joke, as he did every time painful subjects were broached.

Death, time. He'd just highlighted the reasons why I had to write this book. And quickly, before it was too late. So that he shouldn't pass away taking his secrets, his story with him, so that the questions his life raised should not remain unanswered.

It took me two years of research and some twenty interviews before I got to know Adolfo Kaminsky, who I only knew as 'Papa':

decoding his silences, detecting between the notes of his monotone delivery things he didn't put into words, understanding the parables and finding the messages hidden beneath the series of anecdotes that filled my notebook. And sometimes I needed to see the way other people looked at him to understand his choices, his life as a forger, his work underground, his political commitments, his inability to understand society and the hatred motivating various groups that encumbered it, his desire to build a world of justice and freedom.

1

PARIS, JANUARY 1944. When I get to the entrance of the Métro at Saint-Germain-des-Prés, I hurry down without wasting any time. I need to get to the eastern part of Paris, a train heading for Père-Lachaise. I choose a folding seat, keeping away from the other passengers. I have something precious in my attaché case, which I clutch to my chest. I tick off the stations mentally as they pass. République, only three to go. There's noise, voices coming from the next car. The train has been whistling for several seconds now, but the doors aren't closing. The sound of voices is replaced by footsteps, loud, sharp, very distinctive. I recognize them at once. A burning sensation sears my chest at the very moment a Militia patrol, with their armbands and their berets pulled down tight over close-shaven heads, bursts into the car. A sign to the driver and the doors close.

"Identity check! Have all bags ready to be searched."

I don't look around at them. I wait my turn right at the end of the car. I've been used to police checks for ages now, but today I'm frightened.

Keep calm, conceal my emotions. Above all, they mustn't give me away, not today, not now. Stop my foot from tapping out the imaginary rhythm of a frenzied tune. Stop that drop of sweat from running down my forehead. Stop the blood from pounding through my veins. Slow down my heartbeat. Breathe slowly. Hide my fear. Stoical.

Everything's fine. I have a mission to carry out. Nothing's impossible.

Back there, just behind me, they're inspecting identity cards, rummaging through bags. I have to get off at the next stop. There's a militiaman guarding each door; it's obvious I have no chance of avoiding the check, so I get up and go, confidently, to show my papers to the militiaman who's making his way toward me, waving my hand to show that I have to get off soon. He reads the details on my card out loud, 'Julien Keller, seventeen, dyer, born in Ain, Creuse département...' He turns it over and over to examine it from all sides, looking up now and then to observe my reaction with his little suspicious eyes. I remain calm, I know he can't see how afraid I am. I also know, and I'm sure of it, that my papers are in order—I was the one who fabricated them.

"Papers in order... Keller, is that Alsatian?"

"Yes."

"And what have you got in there?"

That's exactly what I wanted to avoid. The militiaman points to the attaché case I'm holding, my hand clutching the handle nervously. For a brief moment I think I can feel the ground giving way beneath me. I'd like to take to my heels and clear off, but any attempt to flee would be futile. A wave of panic makes my blood run cold. I have to improvise, and do it quickly.

"Are you deaf? What have you got in there?" the militiaman asks, raising his voice a little.

"My sandwiches. Do you want to see them?" Suiting the action to the word, I open my attaché case.

No problem, there are some sandwiches inside. They just have to conceal the things I have to hide at all costs. After a moment's hesitation, the militiaman gives me a hard look, scanning my face, searching for any weakness. So I give him my most inane smile, something I've always been able to do when necessary: to look very stupid. The following seconds seem like hours. We've reached Père-Lachaise station, and the train is whistling to indicate the doors are going to close.

"OK, you can go."

I remember very well the shrill whistle of the wind over the graves in the cemetery. Sitting on a bench by one of the paths in the Père-Lachaise, I hadn't come to sit and meditate. My teeth were chattering, my body trembling. I'd had to get out of the metro and drag myself to the cemetery in order to find the solitude I needed to pull myself together again and allow the feelings I'd kept hidden beneath an apparent calm to resurface. I called that the retrospective shock: the body ridding itself of repressed emotions. I just had to wait patiently for my pulse to get back down to normal, for my hands to stop clenching, to relax. How long did it take? I don't know. Five or ten minutes perhaps. Enough time for me to get cold and collect my thoughts. Enough time for me to remember why and for whom I was there, taking risks, and to remind myself how urgent the deliveries were that I was to make. It was this sense of urgency that finally pulled me out of my stupor in the oppressive silence of the cemetery, reminding me that I hadn't a minute to lose. No time to feel despair or self-pity, afraid or discouraged.

I get ready to set off again. Before I get up, I open my attaché case, taking every precaution, for one final check. I lift up the sandwich. Everything's still there. My treasures. Fifty blank French identity cards, my pen, my ink, my rubber stamp and a stapler.

On that day, as on so many others before, I knock at all the doors on a list I was given the previous day and that I've spent the night learning by heart: the names and addresses of dozens of Jewish families who, according to what the network has learned thanks to sympathizers who've infiltrated the bureaucracy, are to be rounded up at dawn. I go up the Boulevard de Ménilmontant then take the Rue des Couronnes to get to the alleys behind the Boulevard de Belleville. Each time new faces are superimposed on these unknown names. Rue du Moulin-Joly, the Blumenthal family, Maurice, Lucie and their children, Jean, Éliane and Véra, have taken the forged papers, now their life underground is beginning.

In the best cases they already have passport photos, I just have to staple them to the blank identity cards then carefully fill them out in the handwriting of a city hall clerk. Sometimes they're happy to take the forged papers but haven't got the necessary materials needed to complete them on the spot. Nevertheless, they take my visit seriously and assure me they won't be at home the next day at the time the roundup is to take place. Some have an uncle, a girlfriend, a cousin where they can hide. Others have no one.

There are some who refuse at first, then change their minds when I assure them it's a free offer. But unfortunately not everyone is so easy to convince. That evening, for example, there was Madame Drawda, Rue Oberkampf. A widow who astounded me by her lack of awareness, her obstinate insistence about seeing me as someone dishonest.

4

When I offered her the papers, she was offended: "Why should I hide, I who've done nothing, who've been French for several generations?" I had time to see, over her shoulder, the table set in the parlor with four children around it, quietly eating their supper. I did everything I could to try and convince her. I explained that my network made it their business to hide children, they would be in an absolutely secure place, with decent people, out in the country, and she would even get news of them. Begging her got me nowhere; she simply wasn't listening, didn't want to hear what I was saying, just stood there looking indignant. What really struck me was that after having listened to me telling her what I'd seen with my own eyes when I was interned in Drancy, the thousands of deportees, whole trainloads being sent to their death, she coldly replied that the death camps didn't exist, that she didn't believe the lies of Anglo-American propaganda. Then, after pausing for a second, she became threatening and warned me that if I didn't leave immediately, she would call the police. Had she not realized that the police, the ones who would come to arrest her and her children in the morning, would not be coming to protect them?

With my case and my sorrow as a double burden, I continued on my way, from door to door, counting and making lists in my head, the future clandestine Jews on the one hand, the deportees on the other. I knew already that I would always remember the latter, that I would never be entirely able to erase their names, their faces from my memory. That I would have nightmares about them. Well aware that I was perhaps the last witness of their freedom, I tried to make a little space for them in my memories.

It was no use hurrying, the glacial darkness of winter nights had finally swept away the clear February sun. After the last door of the last address had closed behind me, it was long past the time of the curfew. I had to turn into a shadow, hug the walls, avoid the light of the street lamps, muffle my steps, glide over the ground and disappear. But above all, I had to find a telephone booth to let my contact know I'd finished my sector: dial a number, leave a coded message, and only then could I go home.

After twenty minutes of walking anxiously, I finally saw in the distance the outlines of the brick building of the Young Men's Hostel, nowadays the Women's Refuge. At that time, it was a hostel for students and young workers. It was very cheap, and I lodged there until I could find something better. When I got to the barred entrance I rang the bell several times, but no one came to open up. I was cold, my feet were frozen, and I was locked out during the curfew. Everywhere in the darkness I thought I could see threatening silhouettes, shadows, hear voices. I felt I was in danger. Nowhere to go.

Exhausted. Having rung the bell one last time, though without deluding myself that anyone might come, I went to hide in the entrance to an apartment block, sitting on a step, hunched up, arms wrapped around me, waiting for daybreak. Unable to get a wink of sleep, startled by every gust of wind, I thought back to Madame Drawda, to all those I hadn't managed to convince, to the children especially. I felt guilty without being able to say of what. I regretted not having been able to find the right words, convincing arguments. I wanted to continue to believe that my efforts, like those of my comrades, had not been in vain. Never give up. I wondered whether Otter had managed to finish his round before the curfew, whether he'd been able to hand out more papers than me. I hoped he hadn't been arrested, for if he had it meant he was already dead. It was January 1944. Contrary to what it said on my papers, I wasn't seventeen, I'd just turned eighteen. I've made myself a year younger in order to avoid the STO.[1] After a childhood that had been abruptly interrupted by the beginning of the war, I still didn't feel entirely grown-up, but from now on I knew for certain that there was nothing of a child about me anymore.

I knew, of course, that all the police were hunting for the Paris forger. I knew that because I'd found a way of producing such a quantity of forged documents that very quickly the whole of the North Zone, as far as Belgium and the Netherlands, was flooded with them. Anyone who needed forged papers in France knew that if they could establish contact with any branch of the Resistance, they would get them immediately. So, obviously, if everyone knew that, then the police did as well. The more we made, the more we had to redouble our precautions. The main advantage I had over the police was that they were probably looking for a 'professional' with machines, printing presses, a wood pulp factory; none of them could have suspected at the time that the forger they were after was nothing but a boy.

Obviously—and fortunately—I was not alone. The man in charge of the laboratory was called Sam Kugiel; he was twenty-four. We called him by his nickname, 'Otter'. The person who'd formerly been in charge and had given that up in order to deal with the convoys of children and frontier crossings was Renée Gluck, alias 'Water Lily', a chemist who was also twenty-four. Both of them had taken their aliases from the names they'd had when they'd belonged to the Jewish Scouts of France (EEIF),[2] where

1. Service du travail obligatoire—the Compulsory Labor Service under which hundreds of thousands of French workers were compelled to enlist and were sent to Germany as forced labor.

2. The Jewish Scouts of France, the Éclaireuses et éclaireurs israélites de France, known as the EEIF or the EIF. [MM]

they'd met before the war. In the laboratory there were also Suzie and Herta Schidlof, sisters who were twenty and twenty-one, students at the Beaux-Arts who made a particularly valuable contribution, as much for their hard work as for their eternal good humor. That was the set-up at the laboratory for forged papers of the '6th' you've heard so much about, a secret section of the UGIF.[3] No one outside the five of us knew the address of the laboratory; even our leaders were kept in ignorance of the secret. On no account should they know, and by strictly respecting this rule we were confident of avoiding getting caught up in lots of disasters.

As cover we pretended to be painters. Our laboratory for forged papers was in a narrow little attic room on the top floor of number 17, Rue des Saints-Pères, which we had transformed into an artist's studio. It was tiny, hardly fifteen square meters, but thanks to a skylight we at least enjoyed fine daylight. Two tables placed end to end took up the whole length of the room. On the one: two typewriters; on the other: sheets of blotting paper. On shelves fixed to the wall I had set out all my chemicals and different inks, scrupulously arranged by order of use. And, as we'd put a few brushes next to them, there was nothing to suggest that they weren't cans of paint and solvents. In order to increase our work surface, I'd cobbled together dozens of sliding shelves that went under the two tables. Thus we could dry out a large number of documents at once with nobody the wiser. The other walls were covered in paintings that we'd dashed off ourselves and behind which we hid the forged papers we'd made, until we could hand them over to our liaison agents. Each of us kept to a set timetable, office hours, so as not to arouse the concierge's suspicions, and from time to time we would

---

3. Union générale des Israélites de France—the General Union of French Jews, an organization set up by the Nazis along the same lines as the Jewish Councils formed in occupied central European countries to collaborate in the deportations.

8

arrive with a painter's palette. In that way none of our neighbors came to ask about the smell of the chemicals. The same was true of the man who came to read the electricity meters. Every time he came to the laboratory, he congratulated us on our pictures. As soon as we could no longer hear his footsteps on the stairs, we burst out laughing for, you can believe me, there was nothing remarkable about our paintings.

The particular feature of our network was its having been created at the very heart of the UGIF, a governmental Jewish organization established by the Vichy regime and financed by the money and goods of the Jews that had been requisitioned by the state. Its task was to gather the Jews together; the UGIF placed minors in children's homes, allowed them to go to school and ensured they were given appropriate food, with the result that many thought its motives were honest and genuine. In reality, the French state had found an infallible means of preparing for the systematic deportation of Jews under the cloak of morality by getting ahead of all the other occupied countries with a system of establishing files and using punch-cards: the Jews had no other place to go and, with the ban on working, were all irremediably dependent on the UGIF and residents in its charitably run hostels. Then they were put on file and rounded up almost immediately.

When they discovered that they were unknowingly taking part in all these deportations, some of the UGIF officials decided to create a clandestine section that they financed with some of the funds they had at their disposal. They recruited volunteers, notably from the Jewish Scouts of France because they were young and loyal and were only too keen to join the Resistance. At the beginning they formed the major part of the network. Thus, thanks to its double agents, the 6th had the advantage of prior access to almost all the lists of those who were to be rounded up in the UGIF hostels or elsewhere.

I was the last to join the laboratory of the 6th section, but as soon as I arrived I had to turn all their methods upside down. When Water Lily told me that she removed the *Jew* stamp with absorbent cotton soaked in ordinary correction fluid or bleach that had been boiled and then Suzie re-colored the card with crayons, I almost fainted. Their method was far too risky. I immediately explained that on contact with skin and sweat the writing would reappear in yellow a few days later. And if they didn't neutralize the correction fluid with an alkaline substance, it would continue to eat away at the paper, and the area that had been treated would take on the texture of blotting paper. The identity card would be no use at all. They looked on dumbfounded as I demonstrated my own chemical solutions and showed them how they should go about it from then on. This was very easy for me. I had all this technical knowledge from my experience as a dyer and the hours I'd spent with an expert in the chemistry of milk. Thanks to my apprenticeship in dyeing, I knew how to dye a cotton thread without affecting the woolen thread. Moreover I'd started doing experiments in chemistry when I was fourteen, doing research into erasing so-called 'indelible' inks. Despite years of analyzing them I hadn't found one that worked—you can delete them all.

I was amused by their enthusiastic response. Suzie talked of magic. A few days later Water Lily decided to devote herself to the convoys of children, convinced that the laboratory for forged papers had found its chemical engineer and would have no further need of her services.

That was only the beginning. Subsequently forging documents became more and more complicated, while at the same time the demand for forged papers was growing day by day. When I joined the network, the 6th section was already in close liaison with other Jewish networks, the Mouvement de jeunesse sioniste (MJS), the Organisation juive de combat (OJC), the free clinic in Rue Amelot and the Oeuvre de secours à l'enfance (OSE). Later other networks formed closer links with us; for example, the Mouvement de libération nationale (MLN) took its orders from London and cooperated with Combat, and Libération Nord, but also the communist networks—the Francs-Tireurs et Partisans (FTP) and the Main-d'Oeuvre immigrée (MOI).[4] The unified Resistance was getting organized. A web was being spun between the different networks, and each one used its special skills to combat the deportations and organize the *maquis* units.[5] These interconnections made it possible to exchange crucial information. The Resistance, which until then had consisted of small, isolated initiatives and groups, was gradually acquiring a structure in which the separate units, like the tentacles of an octopus, were becoming interdependent. We became the most resourceful and effective laboratory in France, the only one to have large-scale production capacity, for by that time I'd found techniques that meant we no longer had to falsify existing documents but could produce new ones as genuine as if they came from the government printing office. I converted the paper myself to make it thicker and made my own 'official' rubber stamps.

Here I must add that I didn't have just one lab at my disposal, but two. When Maurice Cachou, who was in charge of forged

---

4. List of organizations: Zionist Youth Movement; Jewish Combat (sometimes "Fighting") Organization; Organization to Save the Children; National Liberation Movement; Liberation North; Irregulars and Partisans, of which MOI, the Immigrant Workers, a resistance organization of immigrant workers from the French Confederation of Trade Unions, was part.

5. The French Resistance that operated mainly in rural areas. [MM]

papers for the MLN, heard of my achievements, he contacted me directly to ask whether I could do photoengraving. At that time, to avoid lengthy journeys with their police checks, I'd left the Young Men's Hostel and had taken a room in another boarding house in Rue Jacob, very close to the 6th's laboratory. I made a pretense of being an amateur photographer, and the boarding-house cook, who'd become fond of me, let me have a room above mine that she kept empty, assuming I was using it for photographic experiments. In fact, it was there that I set up the MLN research laboratory for forged papers.

Another maid's room, but this time one with an address that was absolutely secret, since I was the only person to have access to it. It was there that I converted the paper, at night, and where, thanks to photoengraving processes, I reproduced an endless stream of stamps, letterhead paper and watermarks. All the blank documents came from my Rue Jacob lab. Everything there was improvised, set up with materials salvaged from junk shops and bits and pieces. But by cobbling things together I managed to reproduce highly sophisticated machines, as good as those in real photoengraving studios. Since centrifugal force was the only effective way of spreading the photosensitive fluid on the plates, I invented a centrifuge made from a bicycle wheel. My pipe made an excellent tool for smoothing out documents impaired by acid substances. In fact that was all I used it for—I've never smoked. With converging and diverging lenses and a little semi-transparent mirror, I reproduced a machine used by Leonardo da Vinci that projected a virtual image of the drawing—or stamp—to be reproduced by hand, making a very precise line possible. That was all hand-crafted but very effective! And since I was constantly having to invent things, I spent a lot of sleepless nights.

Every morning, all I had to do was to take the blank documents to the 6th's laboratory to be filled in; it was so close I didn't have to use the metro.

Our services were made available to everyone. Orders poured in. In ever greater numbers. They came from Paris, from the UGIF, from the South Zone, from London. We had to maintain a rhythm of work that verged upon the unmanageable, sometimes up to five hundred documents a week.

In general it was Otter and I who liaised with those who passed on the orders. I remember that, like me, his appearance was naïve and innocent. It was our best cover. He was short, with sandy hair and freckles, a very small nose and an impish look. A babyish, juvenile look—an open sesame to every door. He was the one who was most often in contact with the Jewish networks; I with the MLN and the communists. But that could change, depending on emergencies. In general we arranged our rendezvous in some busy part of Paris, preferably with a woman. We would meet appearing to be lovers on a date. I always arrived first, each time carrying a rose. Then my 'fiancée' and I would 'go for a walk' together, making sure we exchanged affectionate glances whenever we felt we might be being observed. By the time we separated we both knew what we had to do.

That day my rendezvous wasn't with one of my lady loves but with Marc Hamon, alias 'Penguin', the man who'd recruited me when I joined the Resistance; he too was a member of the EIF.

I knew that if Penguin was coming in person, it must be because his problem was so urgent that he couldn't wait until one of the young women in the network was available. We were to meet in the Tuileries garden. When I arrived I found him sitting on a bench looking particularly tired and worried. I commented that he had lost weight since we first met, at which he laughed and returned the compliment. Then he started to speak in more serious tones.

"Yesterday Radio London gave us some good news. The German army is retreating on all fronts, and from now on we have all the armies of North Africa on our side. The problem is that the Nazis have decided to speed up the process of clearing out the Jews by preparing a huge roundup over the whole of the territory. In three days time, ten children's homes across Paris are going to be raided simultaneously. I have a list for you. I need everything: ration cards, birth certificates, baptismal certificates, plus identity cards for the adults taking them across the border, their orders and the pass for the whole group."

"How many?"

"How many children? ... More than three hundred."

Three hundred children. That meant more than nine hundred different documents to make. In three days! It was impossible. In general the requests came in bundles of thirty to fifty a day, sometimes a few more. It wasn't the first big challenge I'd faced, but in this case the shock was almost too much for me. As I left Penguin, for the first time I was afraid I might fail. Up to that point I'd always managed, through my accumulation of miscellaneous knowledge, to find almost miraculous solutions to technical problems. The better the documents became, the more I'd needed to invent, to show ingenuity in forging the unforgeable with the limited means at my disposal. But this time it wasn't solutions we needed, but quantity, and I knew that I'd reached the maximum productivity I was capable of already. The hours in a day can't be condensed, and unfortunately they can't be prolonged either. No time to think it over. First of all I had to run over to Rue Jacob to make paper: closely woven, nice and compact, or fine, textured or untextured, depending on the nature of the documents to be made. I had to hurry, the stop-watch was already running, the race was starting. A race against the clock, against death.

When, after having left Penguin, I reach the laboratory, out of breath and clutching my case of documents to be filled out, I find Otter, Suzie and Herta there waiting, faithful to their post. But I'm astonished to see that Water Lily's with them. It's rare to find her at the laboratory now that she's taken up other duties. They all look at me, devastated. As far as the three hundred children are con-cerned, they tell me that they've been informed already, which explains the presence of Water Lily, who's come to give us a hand. But, beyond that, Otter has just received an order from the MOI, which needs papers for its Hungarian unit. They look at me ques-tioningly. What they want to know is: does the lab really have the capacity to meet the challenge?

I put the cardboard boxes with blank documents down on the table and, in the tone the situation demands, give the signal.

"The children come first!" Water Lily adds.

Immediately the lab's a hive of activity: Water Lily at the guil-lotine to trim boards for the cards, Suzie coloring in, Herta filling out, by hand and by typewriter. Only Otter, who usually never joins in the production of the cards but looks after all the admin-istrative details, is going around and around like a lost soul.

"If you want to help, you can start stamping and signing the documents."

He gets to work at once, while I make the papers look older using a machine I made myself: I insert some dust and pencil lead,

15

then turn the handle to make them look dirty and worn, so that they don't look too new or as if they've just come from the printer's. The room is gradually pervaded by the smell of the chemicals mingled with that of sweat. Left, right and center we're trimming, cutting out, stamping, coloring, typing, slaving away in our make-shift document factory. Then we stuff the backs of the mirrors and the false-bottomed drawers full of forged papers. Deep down inside we all know that we haven't much chance of getting there, but we take care not to say it. Everything depends on our will-power. After all, the only thing we have is optimism, our only means of making progress.

When it gets dark and we all go home, I head off to my other laboratory, the one on Rue Jacob. How could I sleep when, in a whole day and with the help of Water Lily and Otter's unexpected contribution, we haven't finished a quarter of the papers for the children? What I can't bear is the thought that at this rate we might perhaps manage to fulfill the order of papers for the chil-dren, but only at the sacrifice of the Hungarians.

Stay awake. For as long as possible. Fight against sleep. It's a simple calculation: in one hour I can make thirty blank docu-ments; if I sleep for an hour, thirty people will die...

After two nights of work—interminable, painstaking work, my eye stuck to the microscope—it's exhaustion that's my worst enemy. I have to hold my breath; forging papers is a meticulous task—your hand mustn't tremble at all. Truly delicate work. Most of all I dread a technical mistake, a little slip, an infinitesimal detail that might escape me. Just a momentary lapse of concentra-tion can be fatal, and the life or death of a human being hangs on every document. I check and recheck every sheet. They're perfect.

16

But the doubt remains. I check them again. The stress has gone, but what is worse, I'm literally nodding off. I get to my feet vigorously to wake myself up, take a few steps, slap myself several times. Then I sit down again. One hour equals thirty lives! I don't have the right to give up. I blink and squint my eyes to clear my vision. Is it my printing that's blurred or my eyes that can't see anymore in the dimness of the darkroom?

The next day the lab in the Rue des Saints-Pères is seething with excitement.

We're approaching the finishing line. At five this afternoon Otter and Water Lily will go off with our finished articles, all that we've had the time to make, the fruit of three days' unremitting labor. This morning we've gotten to more than eight hundred finished documents, and I'm finally starting to feel confident. By always repeating the same movements, furiously, like robots, we're working faster than ever, deftly and without respite. Our clothes are greasy and stink of chemicals, we're dripping with sweat, but there is something new in the air on this day, something intangible in the atmosphere. Euphoria! We count out loud to encourage ourselves: 810, 811, 812... carried along by the rhythmical music of the incessant tap-tap of the typewriters, the smack of the guillotine, the thump of the stamps, the click of the stapler and the rumble of the machine that makes the paper look older.

Intoxicated in the swirl of action, I suddenly see a dark veil pass over my eyes. Then, all of a sudden, it's a total blackout. I blink, squint my eyes, feel my eyelids. Still nothing. Blind. My hearing's been taken over by a continuous buzzing, my hands are numb. Suddenly I feel myself lose control of my body.

It seems there was a great crash when I collapsed and tumbled to the ground.

When I woke up, my head was on the floor and all I could see was dark patches. Water Lily took me to one of the network's liaison agents who lived nearby to look after me. I was so afraid that without me the documents wouldn't be completed in time, that I insisted they shouldn't let me sleep for more than one hour. I remember something Water Lily said then that has fixed within me the sense of responsibility for the lives of others: "We need a forger, Adolphe, not another corpse."

2

"*HOW DOES one become a forger?*"

"Why? Is it a job opportunity you're interested in?"

How does one become a forger? I'd say... by chance. Well, not entirely. It turned out that during the years before I joined the Resistance I'd unwittingly accumulated all the knowledge I would need. After that, all I had to do was to apply it.

Like many adolescents, during the war I dreamed of being in the Resistance. I greatly admired the men who fought in the *maquis*, although I was a pacifist myself, incapable of bearing a gun. Even when I was at elementary school it was my little brother who, stronger and braver than me, stood up for me when there were fights. I was the gentle one of the family, timid, contemplative. I dreamed of being a painter but 'that's not a trade,' they'd tell me. What is certain is that without that situation, without the war, I would have led the most ordinary of lives. I would have been a dyer, at most a chemist.

My training, if I may put it like that, began when I went to live in Vire, in Normandy. I was thirteen.

It wasn't the first time we'd moved. The history of my family is typical of that of most Eastern European Jews during those years: a history of repeatedly being exiled, often by force. My parents, both of them Russian, met in Paris in 1916. My mother had fled the pogroms and chosen the 'country of the rights of man'. As for my father, he never told us the reasons for his coming to France, but I know that he was a journalist for the newspaper of the Bund,[1] and I'm sure it was his sympathy with Marxist ideology that had forced him into exile. In 1917, when the Bolsheviks seized power in Russia, the French government ordered the immediate expulsion of all Russian nationals who were considered to be 'reds'. As a former member of the Bund, my father was on their lists. In the middle of the First World War it was impossible to return to Russia, and that is how my parents ended up in Argentina. My brothers and I were born in Buenos Aires, and the whole family obtained Argentine nationality. I was less than five when my parents decided to return to Paris.

In 1938 we went to live in Normandy with my Uncle Léon, my mother's younger brother. He was a complex personality, a self-made man who'd come up the hard way and who, though he could appear extremely irritable, finicky, sometimes even tyrannical, was infinitely kind and devoted to us. He was the one who'd paid for our move to France, who'd found work for my father in Paris and even our accommodation. He had no children of his own and since, in his mind, a house without bursts of laughter and uproarious merriment was synonymous with sadness, he'd had a huge house built, cut into two identical halves in the hope that one day we would come to live there. The events of 1938, the annexation of Austria by Germany and the reports of the tracking down of the Jews, indicated the imminence of war and sped up our reunion. Clearly the capital was becoming too dangerous for a family such as ours, both foreign and Jewish.

And it's true that during the first years of the war we were

1. The general union of Jewish workers in Russia, Lithuania and Poland.

protected in Vire. The people there made us welcome, partly because of my uncle's reputation as an honest stall-holder. Out there everyone knew and respected him. He'd become French because he'd volunteered during the 1914-18 war, in which he'd lost one of his lungs.

At that time, I had the only diploma I ever obtained in my whole life, the certificate attesting that I had completed elementary school. As I was still under fourteen, they sent me to school until I was old enough to leave. The fact that I came from Paris gave me a special status in Vire. At school the boys admired me. And, I may add, the girls, with whom I took the path to the school across the countryside, singing rounds.

There was one, Dora Augier, who was very timid and always stayed close to me. I liked her a lot, but I was careful to avoid running into her father, an old man who looked like a pirate captain because of his wooden leg.

There was another boy who, like me, already had his certificate. This was Bragantti, a lively, impish little Italian with whom I immediately hit it off. Since we'd already finished the curriculum the principal, M. Madeline, who didn't want to let us spend the whole year getting bored, suggested setting up a school cooperative and using the money for the two of us to create a school newspaper. We bought a cheap old printing press and salvaged worn block letters and out-of-fashion fonts from printers as well as from the regional daily paper, which was not unhappy to get rid of them while at the same time doing something for the school. It was both educational and fun, and lucrative as well. We sold the newspaper in order to top up the fund and to buy new, more efficient equipment.

Bragantti and I spent the school year discovering the principles of typography, the means of printing drawings in the desired quantity, and engraving. At the early age of thirteen I was already fascinated by printing.

My elder brother Paul was old enough to go out to work and my parents had decided that, to thank my uncle for his generosity, Paul would help him at the markets. Léon sold hosiery in the squares of the towns in the area. The problem was that they both had quick tempers, and Léon was not used to someone standing up to him. There was one argument after another, and the whole house suffered from their quarrels. In order to calm things down, my mother decided one day that, since I already had my certificate and was more docile, I would leave school and replace Paul. A nightmare for me, who has always been allergic to commerce and now had to abandon the enjoyable school print room, and that's not to mention that my uncle had the annoying habit of rebuking his assistants with a kick in the butt. In time, I would've certainly been able to become reconciled to selling, but the public humiliation on the other hand, no, definitely not.

After a few weeks out in the cold being ill-treated by Léon, I ran off to get myself taken on at the factory on the corner—even lying about my age, since I wasn't fourteen yet. The Société générale électrique made airplane instrument panels for the French army. I would have accepted anything rather than the markets. And it turned out that I liked the factory pretty well. It was a new world for me where I met people who were to be important for my life. As I was young, I was taken on as an apprentice, and I was put in the wiring section, with the women. Aha, I can see you're smiling. You're going to be disappointed—they were all much older than me; I had no chance at all. On the other hand, they confided in me, and I took that very seriously. I learned a lot.

There was one who was sweet, she must have been about twenty. Cécile. She was roguish and funny.

And she smoked. She'd say, "You're not a man yet, so I can tell you things. If you were older it'd be improper..." Or then, "Come and give me a kiss, Adolphe. Here, on my lips, you're not very cuddly, are you..." and she'd burst out laughing. I think it amused her to debauch me a little.

There were also a few men who became my friends. Jacques, a country guy, and Jean Bayer, a redhead from the north, very politically aware, who impressed me a lot because he'd been in prison for hitting his alcoholic father over the head with a hammer when he was beating his wife. He sang Tino Rossi songs and, above all, the songs of the Commune,[2] revolutionary songs. He was a rebel. He had the charisma I dreamed of while I was still at the stage where I was trying to develop a confident demeanor. At the factory I learned to see myself as a grown-up. Now don't laugh. The whole of my adolescence lies in those few months I spent there. I discovered politics. And there I was free and independent for the first time. That's why it's important.

Then, one day, they arrived. It was June 1940. I'd bought a bicycle for the eight kilometers to the factory. Paul—who, like me, refused to submit to Léon's fits of rage—had come to join me there, but in a different section. I was concentrating on trying to beat my bicycle speed record when I saw them coming toward me on the Vire road. The tanks.

Brand new, as if they'd just rolled off the production line. And the soldiers all in gleaming boots and impeccable uniforms. Then I understood what my father meant when, seeing the French

---

2. An uprising in Paris following the French defeat in the 1870-71 Franco-Prussian War. [MM]

draftees in their uniforms that didn't match, some without helmets, he said, "This time it's certain. We've had it, we're not going to win the war with an army like that."

I was alone on the road, face to face with them. I immediately turned around and pedaled off as fast as I could. I hadn't realized they were so close. For me the threat was still far off, even though at the outbreak of the war I'd seen hundreds of refugees, transporting all their possessions along the roads as they fled before the German army. They came from Belgium and the north of France. We'd even put some up and they'd told us about their interminable march, interspersed with bombardments. Then they'd left, heading for another unknown destination. But we hadn't moved. Once Léon had loaded the truck, ready to pack up and leave, but eventually he'd changed his mind, thinking there'd always be time to go later on. Everyone refused to believe the war would drag on like this.

Once the Germans arrived, the factory closed down then reopened some time later to work for German aviation, with a ban on employing Jews. As for Jews, there were only two of us. Paul and I were thrown out. As we were being taken to the door, I heard a voice from behind the work benches: "London calling, London calling. Radio Paris is lying..."

I immediately recognized the voice of my friend Jean Bayer, who, in his own way, was showing his solidarity with us. Some women applauded us, some workers whistled in protest, but the foremen quickly stopped the racket. The war had arrived in Vire.

Rather than going back to working the markets, I quickly replied to an advertisement for an apprentice dyer. M. Boussemard was a chemical engineer, a former NCO in the French army who'd been demobilized for health reasons. He took me on to replace his

24

assistant, who was a prisoner of war. At first he felt I was so young that my work was limited to lighting the boiler, but I very quickly extended my duties. There were shortages of everything and, since it was difficult to find reasonably priced clothes, what we most often had to dye were military uniforms and greatcoats from the '14-'18 War, which we had to change from khaki to brown or navy blue to turn them into civilian clothes. Hard, tiring work, especially in winter. Each item had to be rinsed out in the river when the weather was icy. My own clothes would freeze on me and my hands were numb with cold, but I was being paid and, above all, it was there that I made my first chemical experiments. When the dye was put into the tub where the clothes were soaking, the water turned quite black but, as I was dumbfounded to see, once the process was finished the piece of clothing was black all right but the water was clear as spring water again.

That was when the penny dropped. All of the dye had fixed on the textile, not on the water. "And that," Boussemard explained, "is what shows that the operation has been successful." Fascinated, I asked him if I could have some samples of dye to experiment on the offcuts lying around in my father's workshop—he worked from home as a tailor's assistant. Every day, as we stirred the clothes in the tub, I would ask more questions, and in the evenings I did my experiments in secret. I'd found my vocation. Boussemard was amused by my interest in chemistry and my dogged determination: "So far I've had employees who were happy just to do their work well. With you I have to talk all the time," he grumbled.

Despite his slightly uncouth manner, he was flattered that for once someone was interested in his knowledge. He explained the chemistry to me in the way you would pass on recipes. With him everything was simple. So you see, if I became interested in the effacing of inks, it was initially as a good dyer, to remove stains from the clothes.

I immediately realized that you could do anything, as long as you were determined and found the right method. I quickly had proof of that. As you know, my first researches were into indelible inks, all of which I managed to delete. From then on at the dyer's I became the one to deal with difficult, if not impossible orders. From towns all around people would come to me with stained lace communion gloves, silk wedding dresses. Anything that was supposedly beyond repair was my remit.

The recurrent problem for the enthusiastic beginner in chemistry is dealing with material damage. At first I used the family kitchen for my experiments, the pans and my mother's laundry boiler. But after a few mishaps, notably several explosions, one of which started a fire, chemicals were forbidden in the house.

Since I was something of a handyman and had gotten into the habit of doing little jobs for my uncle, I persuaded him to allow me to use his old house, which he'd simply abandoned, for my laboratory.

At that time I used to cycle past the drugstore in Vire every day without taking any notice of it. That was, until I saw something new in the window. There was a chemical laboratory for sale: retorts, balloon-flasks, a coiled condenser, a real treasure of which I didn't even dare to ask the price. During the new few days I went past it again and again; the laboratory was still there. One week later I finally made up my mind to go in. M. Brancourt, the pharmacist, was whistling as he put some bottles away.

"D'you want something, my boy?" he asked, seeing me eyeing the chemical laboratory.

"Err... no, that is, yes, I'd like to know how much it costs."

"What do you want to do with it?"

"Chemistry."

"What kind of chemistry?"

"Every kind. Experiments. I work at the dyer's, and I've already done some experiments on the effacing of inks. Now I'd like to go farther."

He didn't name his price, but it was easy to see that if I wanted all the pieces, it would cost me a fortune. He demonstrated the equipment to me and even other pieces such as a copper vertical microscope I was sure I'd never be in a position to acquire. Out of the corner of his eye, he watched me marvel at every instrument, and he must have taken a liking to me. We talked chemistry. He was very knowledgeable. He had a doctorate in pharmacy.

"Would it be possible to buy the laboratory bit by bit?" I asked timidly.

"If you like, I'll reserve it for you. You can come whenever you've saved enough to treat yourself to one piece."

I saved all my wages and, one after another, the different components of the laboratory went to my uncle's old house. Brancourt sold them to me at prices that were one-tenth of their true value and even made a gift of the magnificent microscope, which I would never have been able to afford. In my free time I poured over whole books of chemical formulae. In the flea market in Vire I even managed to get ahold of a first edition of the treatise by Marcellin Berthelot, one of the fathers of chemistry. I devoured everything I could find, right down to the practical advice in the *Revue des chaumières* (Cottage Review), in which I found thousands of very effective traditional tricks of the trade.

To perfect my knowledge, I also went once a week to assist the chemist of the butter-dairy—without pay, and in return he gave me his theoretical knowledge and a little slab of butter. The producers who sold their cream to the dairy were paid according to the level of fat content. The volume or weight meant little, only the fat content counted, which meant they avoided possible cheating by crafty farmers who might add water to their cream. What we had to do wasn't very complicated. We just dissolved some methylene blue in a sample of the cream and calculated how long it took for the lactic acid to make it lose the color. That seems a pretty trivial piece of information to you, doesn't it? To me as well, at the time I would never have suspected it would be thanks to that knowledge that I would be recruited by the Resistance.

Apart from being sacked by the factory, little had changed since the Germans had arrived. The war was still going on, yet it seemed to be happening far away, not really affecting us. There had been no obstacles put in the way of the German soldiers and they behaved in a civilized manner, paying without ever complaining. The storekeepers and tradesmen were delighted.

There were, of course, the first Vichy laws. We were no longer allowed to have a post office account nor a savings bankbook. Under the edict of October 3, 1940, we had to register with the police. I remember going with my father for that. We were well known in the region, partly because of my uncle's good reputation. The police clerk explained that as Argentines we were not subject to the requirement to declare ourselves Jews. But my father was keen to be irreproachable in fulfilling his civic duty toward France. I sensed that the clerk wasn't in a hurry to register us, and was insistent about trying to get us to leave. In vain. He added our surnames, first names, dates of birth and address to his file. A few days later we ran into the police clerk in the street. In friendly tones, with a little smile on his lips, he said to my father, "Monsieur Kaminsky, I've lost your files, or perhaps they fell into my stove."

"I'll come in tomorrow to reregister,"

"But there's no obligation."

"Oh but I must. I'll see you tomorrow."

This time we were put on file. As far as wearing the star was concerned, my father was less scrupulous. "If our nationality spares us the obligation, then we won't wear it," he declared.

Eventually, however, the distressing events began to happen, though not exactly where you'd expect. One Sunday the Demoys, the couple who owned the town's brothel, knocked at the door of the family home accompanied by a German officer. They wanted to 'inspect' the house. My uncle, no little proud of his fine residence, didn't need to be asked twice. But then when they were upstairs, in the bedrooms, I heard howls of rage, and I saw Léon kick the German officer in the butt, sending him tumbling down the stairs in a thunderous clatter. From experience I could well appreciate Uncle Léon's kicks. If it had been one of the Demoys who'd received it, I would have laughed, but as it was, I was terrified. On the doorstep my uncle bellowed, "My house a brothel?! Never!"

During the next few days I anxiously awaited the consequences of the incident. For a whole month nothing happened. Then, one evening, two policemen, longstanding friends of Léon, arrived with the disastrous news. The fact that they were in civilian clothes was an ominous sign.

"Kiki, they're coming to arrest you tomorrow morning. You've got to get out of here."

"Where to?"

"Anywhere you like as long as it's somewhere far away."

My uncle left, without a suitcase, hardly with the basic necessities. He took the first train to Paris.

A few weeks later the same policemen came to see us again. They wanted to warn my mother that the Gestapo had intercepted a letter she'd posted to her brother. They had his address in Paris. I know what you're thinking. How could they be so naïve and continue to write to each other? I still can't explain it. They were completely oblivious of what was happening.

We didn't have a telephone. My mother also took the train to warn him before it was too late. "I'll be coming right back. 'Bye kids." Then life went on again, with all the little problems of daily routine. The shortages. You couldn't find anything anywhere, even the most basic necessities, and stocking up on things was getting more and more difficult. With my chemical lab I now knew how to make soap from carbonate of soda, candles—much in demand because of the power outages—from paraffin, wax polish.

Brancourt, the pharmacist, regularly passed on to me orders for bars of soap to treat scabies, which had reached epidemic proportions in the region. I also found a supplier in Flers who gave me all the products he hadn't managed to sell, which allowed me to distribute the whole of my production free of charge. One day he gave me hundreds of kilos of salt rendered unfit for consumption by the addition of iron oxide.

Everyone was short of pure salt because the Nazis had controlled the sale to stop farmers salting their pork to keep it hidden instead of being requisitioned and sent to Germany. I dissolved the salt and filtered it, allowing the iron oxide, which was heavier than the salt, to form a deposit on the bottom; then I recovered the salt on the surface to let it dry and re-crystallize. A few days later it was pure again. I had such a large quantity to purify that I shared the salt out among the farmers and demonstrated the procedure to them. Everyone was at it, for months on end. Thanks to that, for a good while we were a little less hungry in Vire than elsewhere.

With all this to occupy me on top of my work, I didn't spend much time at home. My mother hadn't come back, and a week later my father and Paul went off to find her. They came back after two days and reassured us. She'd contracted some microbe or other and was in hospital in Paris. Nothing serious, apparently. And then the days passed without them saying anything more about it.

My reputation as a manufacturer of free bars of soap was soon all around town.

The women, in particular were short of it for the washing. I used to go around the houses on my bike, which allowed me to see Dora again, the girl I used to walk to school with. The poor thing had had to give up school to look after her father, who was very ill and, with the passing of time, no longer frightened me. And it was my bars of soap that also kept me in contact with my former colleagues at the factory. I really liked seeing Cécile again. Even though times were hard, she was still as funny as she used to be. Except one time when she greeted me looking really down in the mouth.

"Hi, it's you. Would you like a cig?"

"No thanks, I don't smoke."

"Pooh… It's because you're still not a man. You ought to try it. On my sad days, I smoke even more."

"Sad? Why?"

"You haven't heard?"

"What?"

"Jean Bayer, from the factory."

"What's he done?"

"Gone and gotten himself executed by firing squad."

It was a rainy winter's day at the end of 1940. I left on my bike and pedaled like mad, not going anywhere in particular, across the plain of Normandy. Jean Bayer dead. The first person dear to me that the war had torn away. Him with his cynical jokes, the eternal cigarette butt stuck in the corner of his lips, his offhand manners. I went through all the times I'd spent trying to be like him. I was pedaling against the wind. And then, lost in the tumult of memories, I suddenly realized the worst thing of all. My mother was dead. I realized just like that. A lot of water poured down my cheeks that day, and it wasn't rainwater. It had taken Jean's death to stop me being blind. What illness could have kept her in hospital all this time? Since my father had told us the story about some microbe, he had withdrawn into total silence. How could I not have understood? Even my little sister Pauline, who was only ten, had clearly expressed her concern.

When I got home, I asked my father straight out, and he confessed. The railway company had found her body on the line. She was on her way back from Paris after having warned Léon, who'd disappeared at once. Paul had gone with my father to identify the body, which was why they took two days. Paul had been so traumatized at seeing "her head separated from her body and the bits of brain," that he'd preferred to say nothing to us, the younger ones. But my father ought to have informed us. The detectives carrying out the investigation claimed she'd opened the door of the train while it was traveling, assuming it was the toilet door.

And that's what Paul preferred to believe, and still does today. My father brought in a Parisian lawyer to clear the matter up, but he was a Jew and was arrested and deported not long after. I have nothing but contempt for the accident theory. As far as I'm concerned, she was pushed; it was an assassination.

"But no one can prove it?"

Now you tell me: if someone told you I'd fallen out of the train because I'd confused the outside door with that to the toilets, what would you say?

So there you are. That's just the way it was. Anyway, a few days later something happened that corroborated my view: a letter from the *Kommandantur* ordering us to leave Léon's house, which had been requisitioned by the German Military Administration and allocated to the Demoys for a price fixed by the Mayor's office. The Demoys were taking their revenge. The house, transformed into an officers' brothel, was never empty throughout the war. People say that the drinks and the girls there were delicious, and cheap.

We were allocated accommodation by the Mayor's office, on Place de la Gare with an old lady who had no say in the matter. Almost every day I went to see Brancourt, the pharmacist. After my mother's death I threw myself body and soul into chemistry; it was my only reason for living. Brancourt was ready to help me every time I hit a snag in my research—he gave me loads of advice. But not just that, we talked about everything, especially the war. He was very humane, he was a good listener and gradually he became a kind of father in spirit.

An announcement on Radio London during the summer of 1942 was the first news that gave us some hope. The Battle of Stalingrad. The German army was finally coming up against resistance. I also heard rumors that the sabotage of the German convoys was intensifying, groups were being organized. In response to these attacks, the German Administration decided to requisition all the men in the town to take turns in keeping a watch on the railway lines at night. In a way they were hostages because if there was an attack on the railway, those on watch were executed by firing squad. I wasn't old enough yet but I went all the same in place of my father and Paul, so that I could see Brancourt. I can't say how, but in the course of our discussions I eventually realized that he was an agent for de Gaulle's intelligence service and for which the pharmacy was just a cover. He was in contact with the groups organizing acts of sabotage in the Normandy sector. I didn't want to mourn my dead without doing anything, and he knew that. One night, as we were drinking ersatz coffee and watching the lines while struggling against sleep, he said, "If I showed you how, would you be willing to make some things for me that are a little more dangerous than bars of soap?"

How long had I been waiting for that proposition without daring to mention it out loud!

"Now listen carefully, it's complicated work. You have to take the greatest care about the quantities."

From that day on as well as bars of soap, candles and salt, I made more harmful products that corroded the transmission lines, made railway parts rust, and little detonators as well. Being involved in the sabotage meant that for the first time I didn't feel entirely impotent following the death of my mother and my friend Jean. At least I had the feeling I was avenging them. And I was proud; I was in the Resistance.

3

WHEN THE GERMANS came to arrest me, in the summer of 1943, I was at the dye-works with my younger brother, Angel, whom I had gotten hired. They ordered us to follow them and get into a covered army truck. The rest of my family was already inside, with old Augier and his daughter Dora, the girl I used to walk to school with. A pretty thin roundup: we were all that was left of the Jews of Vire. Seeing my father, I hoped he would say something, anything to reassure me, but there was nothing to say. I did the same as everyone else: didn't protest, didn't say a word. No one asked where we were going. The journey lasted two hours.

The truck finally stopped, and we were all crammed into one cell of La Maladrerie, the much-vaunted model prison in Caen. Seven of us in ten square meters. No room to stretch out to sleep, except for Augier, who was too old and ill. For two days not a single guard came to see us, we had nothing to eat, nothing to drink. We'd been forgotten.

Then Augier, lying on his straw mattress, mouth half open, eyes glued to the ceiling and tears running down his wrinkled cheeks, started to groan. Dora bent over him, but the old man was dying, and his groans grew louder and louder, punctuating each breath. I tried to breathe in the same rhythm, to share his suffering. My father hammered on the door to let the guards know a man was about to die. He made such a racket that an officer eventually came to see what was going on.

"This man fought in the '14-'18 war, beside you, for Germany. He lost a leg in it. You can't let him die in prison."

The officer left without a word. And Augier asked my father to sing the kaddish, in advance. I saw my father get up and recite the prayer for the dead for him. It was the first time I'd ever heard a prayer; in fact I had no idea my father knew any, and in that prison, breaking a silence of several days, the religious texts delivered by my father's voice took on a very special significance. I knew that this prison was but one stage and that at the end there would be camps, perhaps death. Before getting up to sing the prayer, my father looked each of us in the eye. That day it was truly for all of us that Solomon sang.

Augier was freed, but not his daughter. My father promised to look after her as if she were his own, and we took Dora into our family so that she wouldn't be an orphan. The next day we were shoved onto a train with other Jewish prisoners from the region. Full buses 'discharged' their passengers, whom the soldiers pushed into the cars. Hundreds of people, of all ages and all classes, were piled up in them, while from the general hubbub the name of Drancy was already emerging. Paul went round the car, asking everyone, "Has anyone got any paper? Got some paper? A fountain pen?"

Some had been rounded up at home and had brought luggage. From them Paul got what he was looking for and came back to us.

"What are you doing?"

"I'm writing to the Argentine consul."

"What for?"

"Look, they're all wearing the star. Not us. If anyone can do something for us, it's the consul. We're protected."

He wrote several letters. All the same, with our names, the date and where we were being sent, so that Argentina could demand our release. The train departed. Paul handed out the letters to anyone he could, to railway workers, he even threw some out of the window.

All we could hope for was that some kind soul would pay for a stamp and mail them.

Let me describe Drancy. A housing project surrounded by barbed wire. Long, horizontal six-story blocks, unfinished, forming a "U" around a vast square courtyard. No doors. No windows. No partitions. A building site in reinforced concrete left as a skeleton. A prison without walls to protect us from inquisitive eyes and from the cold. Nothing on the horizon besides guards and, above our heads, the menacing shadow of the five gigantic towers, where the German occupation troops were housed.

The Palace of Drafts—in both senses of the word: the wind, of course, but also the drafts of detainees arriving and leaving by the trainload.

There were thousands of us deportees arriving and leaving by the trainload. Forty to a room. Men and women separated at night. An anthill. No one stayed at Drancy. That was where they made their selection before sending the convoys off to the various camps in Europe. Some had barely arrived when they were on their way again. 'The work camps,' the Germans called them. Have you ever seen old men and children scarcely two years old capable of working? It wasn't the beginning of the war any longer. Everyone had heard about the Vel' d'Hiv roundup.[1] And the convoys, as we well knew, all had the same destination: Pitchipoï.[2]

On the evenings before the convoys left, you could hear, echoing throughout the building, the tears of those whose heads had been shaven and who stayed on the stairs because of the lack of beds in the rooms. It sounded like a madhouse. When I heard them I would think of Pauline, my little sister, and Dora in the women's block. All night I just hoped they'd managed to get to sleep, that they had no idea what was happening. Dora. As my father had promised Augier, we had made her one of us. Unfortunately this adoption was only valid for us. No sooner had we arrived than she was put on the lower floor, the one for those who were considered 'deportable'. My father did everything he could to have her recognized as his daughter, he was even granted a meeting with the commander of the camp, Alois Brunner. But Dora was French and Brunner adamant. His response made my father accept the inevitable: "If, as you say, you can't abandon her, I can make room for your whole family in the next convoy."

A few days after that grim interview Dora's name was on the departure list. When she left, there was nothing we could do, and time has not erased the immense feeling of guilt it has left me with.

The others left, we stayed. A thousand per convoy, that was the rule, and Brunner was the kind of man who was punctilious about figures. If a person was missing at the roll call, someone else had to take their place. The camp could be jam-packed one day and almost empty the next, until the inevitable processions of prisoners came

1. A mass roundup of Jews in Paris by the French police in 1942, so named after the Velodrome d'hiver, the Winter Velodrome, where they were gathered. [MM]

2. The name the Jews in Drancy used for the death camps.

to fill it up again. Jews, short, tall, with blond hair, brown hair… It was not until I was at Drancy that I realized I knew nothing about them. There were very few Jews in Vire. The Lévys, who employed my father, the Augiers, ourselves and a few others. Nazi propaganda said awful things about them, gave descriptions that were caricatures in which I didn't recognize myself, and the general population seemed to approve. I'd heard anti-Semitic remarks throughout the war and let them pass without realizing. People would say to me:

"It's the fault of the Jews, those dirty Jews."

"But we're Jews as well."

"Oh, yes, but with you it's not the same, you're like us, While the others…"

Did they even know what the others were like? I had no idea myself. At Drancy I discovered the Jews in all their diversity. I loved them, and through them I came to love myself—I felt I was a Jew, and I've never lost that.

It was at Drancy that I learned algebra and arithmetic from an old gentleman who had taught at the École polytechnique[3] in the days when the Jews still had the right to teach. Every day, he devoted whole hours to me. I was fascinated by the relationship between math and chemistry. I wanted to know everything—I took notes and memorized them during the night in order to be able to go on to the next lesson the following day.

Thanks to that old man, my training in theory could even continue inside the fortress. He was moved by my thirst for knowledge, and I think each of us had a fundamental and irrational need for these lessons because they were the only moments when we could forget our condition as internees. I was his last pupil. One day, when

3. At the time the military academy of artillery and engineering. [MM]

it was time for our classes, he wasn't there. He hadn't wanted to tell me beforehand that his name was on the list, perhaps to spare us a difficult farewell.

My political awareness was also filling out. The interminable conversations I'd had with Jean Bayer in the factory and with Brancourt while guarding the railway lines at Vire continued with Ernest Appenzeller, a young blond man with blue eyes who could have posed for the poster demonstrating the superiority of the Aryan race. I was seventeen, he was eighteen. He said he'd been arrested by mistake. Because he'd been circumcised. "Circumcised but not Jewish," he added.

He was demanding an examination by the German scientific commission that specialized in racial questions, for he was sure they could only conclude he was Aryan. With his determined tone and his quick-wittedness, he reminded me of my friend Jean. He'd often say to me, "If I were a Jew, I'd be a Zionist."

Like my father, I thought that a land for the Jews was a utopia. I felt that, whatever their religious affiliation, everyone ought to feel at home where they lived, and that above all there was no reason why religion and nation had to coincide. There was no subject under the sun Ernest and I didn't talk about. We exchanged our points of view, theorized about everything, politics, philosophy, our ideals. We even talked about theology, that is, he did mainly because I knew nothing about it. I was impressed by his knowledge of Judaism, him not being Jewish. Together we invented a new world. A better world.

In three months I met countless numbers of people, encounters that were marvelous, infinitely enriching. I started so many friendships, only to see my friends leave me, deported, one after the other. And I was powerless to do anything. As an Argentine I had the right to work inside the camp. I was a house painter. On the walls I whitewashed, many things had been written—names, dates, messages that I didn't want to cover up, because they were perhaps the last signs of life of those who'd written them. I was caught in the act of using a bit of iron to re-engrave the inscriptions I'd just painted over. I was sent to work in the laundry to stop me doing 'something stupid' like that again. For some unknown reason Aloïs Brunner, who did an inspection tour of the camp every day, would always stop in front of me, draw himself up to his full height and give me a hard stare. In front of him, we were supposed to lower our eyes. But I didn't. I held his gaze. In the name of Dora and all the rest. Since everyone was going away to die and I was staying there, I couldn't give a damn about the consequences. I'd stopped being afraid. I can still remember Brunner's look, his little, piercing black eyes staring into mine. Every day he would look me up and down, ignore my arrogance and continue on his way without a word. I have no idea why he didn't say anything. I've never understood. Perhaps his curiosity had been aroused by the insistent demands of the Argentine consulate for our release; perhaps it was just because I was called Adolphe.

"How did you all manage to get out of Drancy?"

It was Paul's letters to the Argentine consul that saved us. We spent three months in the camp. That was the maximum. So we owed our survival to the diplomatic cowardice of a government that, in order not to have the powerful North American states against them, without on the other hand breaking off the economic agreements tying them to Nazi Germany, had declared itself neutral. Neutrality doesn't exist. To do nothing, say nothing, is enough to make one an accessory.

When my father told us we were going to be released, I came very close to refusing. To leave while the others were condemned to death. Why us and not them? Solomon managed to convince me that I was no use there, but outside perhaps... I immediately thought of Brancourt and the detonators I made in Vire. My place was up there, at his side. I had to go back, whatever the cost.

So there we were, outside, in Paris, without a dime, with dozens of letters from prisoners in Drancy hidden in the lining of our jackets. The anti-Jewish laws were worse in Paris than anywhere else. We still weren't wearing the yellow star, but our papers had the very conspicuous stamp in red ink. We couldn't go to a hotel, nor return to Normandy, nor even buy ourselves some food. Tough freedom. I hadn't been in Paris since we left to go and live in Vire in 1938. The city had changed a lot. The signposts were all in two languages: German and French. The shop-windows had 'Jews prohibited' notices. Walls were covered in posters with drawings of hook-nosed Jews with big ears and fingernails like claws. German officers drove along the streets in shiny, brand-new cars, forming an outrageous contrast with the shabbiness of impoverished Paris. We had been advised to go to the UGIF. And that, after having wandered around like lost souls until the curfew was approaching without finding anything else, is what we did. We got into the last car of the metro, third class, reserved for Jews. Paul didn't want to do that and went off on his own. He suspected the UGIF hostels were a trap, and he was right. The UGIF was the Jews collaborating with the Nazis.

We were allocated to a former retirement home in Choisy-le-Roi in the Val-de-Marne, where we were fed and looked after. My time at Drancy had left me so thin that I had difficulty standing up, my knees kept giving way. When I'd recovered my strength a bit, I headed straight for the secondhand booksellers on the embankments of the Seine to buy chemistry books. I wanted to find out how to make powerful explosives before going back to put myself at Brancourt's disposal. I'd written to him as soon as we were set free—very matter-of-fact, nothing compromising, obviously—just to let him know I was alive. He replied—it was more than I'd hoped—with a long, warm letter full of encouragement and kindness, in which he reminded me that he'd always be ready to help me whatever the cost. I kept that letter under my pillow so that I wouldn't be without it, even during the night, as a lucky charm.

I'd been there for ten days or so when, in the middle of the night, around four in the morning, I heard the sound of vehicles. The engines were turned off right under my windows. Policemen's steps. In the time it took them to come up the stairs, I swallowed Brancourt's letter. I ate it. It was so long I couldn't finish it, but since I'd managed to get the most important parts down, I threw the rest into the toilet and pulled the chain. The police came into the room and told me I had ten minutes to get ready to leave. I took all my chemistry books, heavy tomes and, since I was still weak, one of them very politely helped me. I told myself the man was carrying the things with which I was trying to fight against him.

Back to Drancy. We're overcome with a horrible feeling that we'd done this all before. This time my father protests as soon as we get there. It seems there's been a mix-up. Some say, "Yes, there's been an order to arrest them," others say there hasn't. Then, finally, we're released after twenty-four hours. And there, outside the exit, we meet a group of people heading for Drancy surrounded by police. My father hears them talking in the mixture of Spanish and Yiddish characteristic of Argentine Jews.

"Where d'you come from," he asks them.

"We're Argentine."

"But... the diplomatic agreement?"

"It's over. They're arresting all the Argentines."

We cleared out. The German-Argentine agreement suspended, goodbye to our shield. We owed our freedom to poor communications between the French police, the SS and the Drancy administration. A few more hours and we'd have had it.

The following day my father disappeared and when he came back, he called a family meeting.

"I've gotten in touch with some very old friends that I hadn't seen for years. From Russia, former members of the Bund. We're going to have to disperse. Each one of us will go their own way."

"Even me?" Pauline, just thirteen, asked with a tremor in her voice, terrified at the idea of separating from us.

"Each of you will be placed on a farm. I don't yet know where or how, but first of all we've got to get some forged papers. We have to give them some passport-size photos, and they want it to be a young person who brings them. I'm counting on you, Adolphe. You have a rendezvous quite soon. Your contact's called Penguin."

Forged papers... I'd been brought up with such respect for the law that I have to admit that hadn't occurred to me before...

A few hours later I arrive at the rendezvous and, following instructions, wait beside the statue of Molière outside the Collège de France, carrying a book. I stand there, among the comings and goings of passers-by, students for the most part, and no one comes. I look around from time to time to see if I can spot someone who corresponds to my idea of a member of the Resistance. I don't know why, but I imagine someone like Jean Bayer, tall, self-assured, relaxed.

"Adolphe."

I turn round and find myself facing a short, slightly tubby young man with dark curly hair. He greets me normally, as if we'd known each other for ages so that there's nothing suspicious about our meeting.

"Penguin?"

He checks there's no one following us then we go into the Collège de France. "You've got the photos?"

I quickly pass them to him, and he stuffs them into his pocket without pausing during our walk through the corridors.

"We're going to try to keep the initials of your real names for the papers. You were born in which year?"

"1925."

"We'll put '26 to make you a bit younger. That way you'll avoid the STO. As for profession, we'll put student."

"No, that's impossible! I have to work to earn my living."

"You have a trade?"

"Yes, I'm a dyer."

At that moment a student brushes past and walks close to us. Penguin changes his tone of voice: "Do you remember her? Lucienne! Just imagine, I saw her again, purely by chance. She's doing law now, and she's still living with her parents..."

The student walks on and Penguin continues. "You said you're a dyer?"

"Yes, that's right."

"So that means you know how to remove ink stains?"

"Yes. That's even my specialty. I'm also doing some chemistry."

"But what about indelible inks?"

"There's no such thing. They can all be removed."

Once more there are students close to us. Penguin looks all around and talks about other things, about a friend I'm supposed to know who can't come to dinner tomorrow because he's got flu. I start to get the idea, and we make small talk before going back to where our discussion broke off.

"We've got a problem with Waterman's blue ink. Impossible to remove it—it stands up to everything. Do you know what we need to do?"

"No. I'd need to analyze it to see what it's composed of."

"That I do know, it's methylene blue."

"In that case it's very simple. You need to use a reducing agent, lactic acid."

"You're sure of that?"

Was I sure? And how! I tell him about the dairy chemistry in Vire, the chemistry books I've devoured, the stains on clothes, the bars of soap, the candles and even the detonators. He looks me up and down, then finally asks the question I've been expecting: "Would you be interested in working for us?"

Two days later I have another rendezvous, same time, same place, to collect the forged papers for my family. From now on I'm Julien Adolphe Keller; Angel and Pauline have the same surname; my father's become Georges Vernet. We're all French born and bred—we've just been 'naturalized' by the services of the Resistance.

Since there are lots of people around, Penguin talks to me about his cousin, who was supposed to be getting married but her fiancé's broken it off, etc, etc... And I'm afraid he's not going to mention the proposition he made me. I've been so excited I haven't been able to sleep for two days. Just as we're separating he tells me to go and take a room at the Young Men's Hostel, a Protestant institution run by the Salvation Army, adding, "We'll be in touch with you."

For three days I was tested to see if I was the kind of person who had a loose tongue. A medical student who also lodged at the Hostel came to see me every evening. He was very nice, or should I say *too* nice... He asked me lots of questions about myself, my memories, my family. Naturally I stuck to the official answers. I was Julien Keller, a dyer, the son of farmers from Lyons. That was all. On the fourth evening he came back with Penguin, who took me to a hotel on Place Maubert where two men were waiting for us in an ordinary room. 'Giraffe' and 'Heron', both of them around twenty-five, were introduced to me by their EIF names. They didn't ask me a single question but made up for it by talking a lot... about me. From what they said, I understood that inquiries had been made and that they knew everything, right down to the death of my mother.

Giraffe asked me to sit down at the desk, placed a blank identity card in front of me with a piece of paper containing all the information to be transferred to the card. All I had to do was to carefully copy out all the details in the handwriting of a little clerk in the mayor's office who'd finished elementary school but nothing more. Anyone could have done it—it was just an initiation ritual, but I was extremely tense, I don't know why. It was my first forgery. I will never forget that somber room, the smell of the wooden desk lit by a little lamp, the pen and the ink-well, and the presence of Penguin, Heron and Giraffe behind me, watching silently over my shoulder. I signed the identity card with a very French name and showed it to them. I had passed the first hurdle, but I was far from suspecting that it was the first step in a long life as a forger.

4

MARCH 1944. After having walked along the Palais-Royal, I'm hardly out of breath when I get to the Hôtel Montpensier. Since I've stopped taking the metro, I've gotten used to walking without getting tired. At reception I ask for M. Lambert. A little lady of indeterminate age gives me the number of a room on the first floor. The doubts that have been tormenting me since I was told about this rendezvous increase as I go up the stairs to the room of the man who calls himself Lambert. If it's a trap, then I'm caught in it.

Well aware that, in wartime, distrust is one of the best means of survival, I go all through the corridor and make a quick analysis to note any possible escape routes I can use if there should be a problem. We're on the first floor. There's an elevator, the stairs and a window looking out onto the street. If I have to run, jumping out of the window would be the best way. At worst I'd be risking a sprained ankle. No security locks, I open the window now, you never know. Outside, the sky is threatening, plunging the city into twilight gloom. One last glance at my watch. It's five o'clock, the time of my rendezvous.

Earlier in the afternoon Otter came to the lab. He was returning from a meeting with Albert Ackerberg, the successor to Jacques Pulvert as head of the 6th section, and he ordered me to take a package of blank demobilization cards to a man I'd never heard anyone mention before, a M. Lambert in the Hôtel Montpensier. I'd found it surprising he didn't take them himself; after all, that was his job. Usually my contacts had EIF 'totem names' unless they were women. To crown it all, the idea of meeting an unknown man in a hotel aroused my most paranoiac instincts. I protested.

"Why aren't you going yourself?"

"It's you he wants to see."

And why did this man want to see me? No idea. I must have shown some anxiety, for Otter felt he needed to reassure me: "Don't worry, he's definitely one of us."

But he said nothing more and went back to immerse himself in his notebooks, so I took the cards and left. So you see, that's what it was like in those days. We didn't talk a lot, and it would have been out of place to question an order.

Room 18. I knock on the door. A soft, grave voice invites me to enter, and I find myself in the charming sitting-room of a hotel suite with bourgeois furnishings. Facing me is a man of around thirty with an intellectual look, tortoiseshell glasses on his nose. "Monsieur Lambert?"

I calm down a little when I detect, deep within his myopic gaze, almost as much distrust as there is in mine. If this man can be afraid of me, it means he certainly hasn't come to arrest me.

The man's expression gradually relaxes until eventually he appears completely at ease. Perhaps it's my frail physique that calms him down or simply the fact that I correspond precisely to the description he's been given.

"Maurice Cachoud," he says in a friendly voice, grasping my hand.

One word and my suspicions fade away. Cachoud, I know that name, and I can certainly confirm that this man is definitely one of us since he's the person in charge of forged papers for the MUR (Mouvements unis de Résistance—Unified Movements of Resistance) in the South Zone. I've heard talk of him many times, but we've never met. I knew that he was based in Nice; in fact, we've corresponded on technical matters. Otter often asks me to note down my latest discoveries so he can send them to the other laboratories for forged papers, the most important of which are those in Grenoble and Nice. I've also heard rumors that, since the recent creation of the MLN, Cachoud has been responsible for centralizing the orders for forged papers on a national level, bringing all the networks together and that, in a certain way, makes him my ultimate superior in the hierarchy. To meet him in this way, without intermediaries and, what is more, at his request, is not a trivial matter. That is the moment at which I realize that I've just started to play in the major leagues.

Cachoud invites me to sit in one of the armchairs around a small, low table. I pretend not to be impressed and make an effort to appear as relaxed as possible. As I'm making myself comfortable I see a head going past the half-open door to the bedroom. The head glances at us but then disappears without being introduced. I hardly had time to do more than make out a silhouette. Given its broad shoulders, it must be his bodyguard. Back in the sitting room, Cachoud comes straight out with the reasons why he's gotten me to come.

"I've heard a lot about you and your skills," he says.

50

Embarrassed, wavering between modesty and pride, I stammer that all I do is apply the things I've learned in chemistry and dying.

"Do you know of an invisible ink that can be used for correspondence?"

A ridiculous question from one forger to another. Of course I know of one, of several even. Nor is there any doubt that he must know lots about them himself. Deciding that the question must have been asked to test my knowledge, I play along and start scribbling down six formulas for invisible ink. At that moment the strapping man I glimpsed earlier on bursts into the room and goes to lean against the wall a bit farther away. Concentrating on the formulas, I don't pay particular attention to him, but I do notice that the way he holds his head and his assured gait are not entirely unfamiliar. To me he seems to have a much too lordly air for a bodyguard, a distinctive sophistication mingled with much too much arrogance for my taste. If I admire his elegance, I don't at all like the way he's looking me up and down.

I concentrate on my formulas, bending over my pen, and I sense him quietly come closer. When I look up he's very close and leans over me.

"What's your name?" he asks in a voice of authority.

"Julien."

"Yes, but your surname, what's that?"

"Keller."

A few seconds pass. As I continue to write down the formulas for my inks, I can sense his insupportable scrutiny that is still fixed on me. He comes even closer, so close that our noses are almost touching. He peers at me, examines me; if he could do it with a magnifying glass I'm sure he would. I'm about to stand up, close to breaking point, when he exclaims, "Adolphe?!"

I almost have a heart attack. No one besides the people in the laboratory can know my first name.

"Adolphe Kaminsky," he goes on, his face a picture of astonishment, "Drancy!"

I stare, wide-eyed, at this odd fellow, then finally I recognize him: "Ernest Appenzeller!"

"Well I never!" he bellows, smacking the table, "So this 'specialist' is you!"

Ernest, how could I not recognize him? And that, yes, what a surprise! Ernest, the man who's 'circumcised but not Jewish', has changed his Drancy rags for a new suit, and the metamorphosis is so great that I'm completely flabbergasted. I stand there, dumbfounded, looking at him from head to toe while he moves his large body in sweeping gestures, all the time repeating the same words, like a scratched record: "Well I never!"

In the three months we spent in Drancy, my family and I were the only ones to be released from the camp. And Ernest, who when we left was still denying he was Jewish, had only his silver tongue and his boyish good looks going for him. The likelihood of us seeing each other again was pretty remote.

"You're in the 6th?"

"Yes. And you, you're MLN?"

"No, I'm with the MJS, attached to the OJC, the Jewish Combat Organization," he says with pride in his voice.

Combat was Ernest's favorite word. Now I recalled all the times at Drancy when he'd said to me, "If I were a Jew I'd be a Zionist," "if I were a Jew, I'd take up arms, go and fight with the *maquis*." I also remembered the scorn he displayed for all those who'd quietly accepted wearing the star, all those who'd docilely gone to be registered in the mayor's office, imagining that their civic obedience would guarantee their survival. And wasn't that what my father and I had done? Ernest used to say that if the Jews had been persecuted since time immemorial, it was quite simply because they were the ideal victims because of their attitude of resignation, submission, and their aversion to combat. Ernest clicks his fingers, and a roguish smile appears on his lips as he takes a document with the Reich letterhead out of a drawer. "I really fooled you in Drancy, eh? And them too, those morons of the Scientific Commission. And Brunner, you should have seen the expression on his face when I showed him this document. Look."

He hands me a letter from the Scientific Commission, personally signed by the famous Professor Montandon: his certificate of Aryan descent, attesting that after a detailed examination Ernest corresponds to all the criteria of the Aryan race besides, of course, the minor detail of his missing foreskin, due to a phimosis, as the certificate states. Yes, he really did fool me. Like everyone else I believed his story of an operation. And the most unbelievable part of his story is that, in order to have his case examined by the Commission, he had to append both a birth certificate and a certificate of baptism to his file. And I was the one who fabricated those certificates in the lab of the 6th section, without knowing whom they were for! We have so much to tell each other! And from now on there's something binding us. Like me, Ernest saw the thousands of shorn heads in Drancy and heard the moans during the nights. That brings us even closer together.

Thus it is that I learn that Ernest is not only Jewish but the son of an Austrian Rabbi, has been underground since he was thirteen and a Resistance fighter for the same length of time. At first a young marksman, notable for his exceptional coolness, Ernest quickly rose through the ranks until he was entrusted with terrorist missions against the Nazis. Having become one of the elite agents in France; he then headed a team of marksmen, organizing and supervising targeted assassinations. Ernest, the 'killer' of the network, was equally expert at silencing informers. "You just have to eliminate one or two," he tells me, firing a pretend pistol to illustrate his point, "and the others eventually hold their tongues if they don't want to be bumped off as well."

Ernest's ringing laughter gradually fades into silence. Cachoud has observed our joyous reunion dumbfounded, and the business of the invisible inks is forgotten. We go on to more serious matters. As for Ernest, this isn't his field. After all the agitation at the start of the meeting, he sits there in silence, religiously puffing away at his pipe, forming an 'O' with his lips and emitting little smoke rings. Cocooned in the plush hotel suite, Cachoud subjects me to an interrogation on technical matters. "Do you know how to reproduce imprinted watermarks? Relief stamps? Remove the ink on documents without affecting the color the paper has taken on with age? Make new paper look as if it's old?..."

I answer yes to all his questions. Even if sometimes I don't know precisely how to do what they are asking, convinced that nothing's impossible, I tell myself that if I rack my brains I'll find something. And I always have.

I wonder where these questions are going to take us; I have the feeling they're just a prelude to some more complicated request. And indeed, after a while Cachoud breaks off and puts his hands together in front of his lips as a sign of reflection.

"We have a problem with our photoengraver in Paris. Until recently he did the work without delay, then he slowed down his production and now he's told us he's stopping because he's afraid

his staff might be watching him. It's a hard blow for the Resistance...
You, who know how to do everything, could you set up a photoengraving studio?"

I know nothing at all about photoengraving, but I do know my ability to learn quickly so, just as to all his other questions, I answer yes, though on one condition: that I can have a short period of training with the photoengraver in question.

"My assistant René Polski will arrange that for you."

I leave the meeting with an order for demobilization cards to be printed—as usual it's a matter of urgency, of course—and for a photoengraving laboratory to set up. Cachoud can return to Nice, satisfied with our discussion. Now he was going to be traveling between Nice and Paris until he settled permanently in Paris several months later, which meant that we'd be seeing each other a good few times.

On my way home I head for the embankment to look for a book on photoengraving. On the stall of a freezing bookseller I find the two volumes of L. P. Clerc's *Photography Theory and Practice* that was to be my bedside reading for the next few days.

The next day I knocked at the door of M. Goumard's photoengraving studio in Rue Saint-Denis.

"Let's go to my office, it'll be quiet in there," the thin, stern-looking little man whispered; I put his age at about fifty.

We crossed the room where a good dozen men were busy on colossal machines. A veritable factory: a work table with arc-lamps, etching trays, engraving tanks, agitating tubs, inking rollers. If that was what a photoengraving studio was like, I was going to have difficulty fulfilling Cachoud's request.

Goumard ushered me into a windowless office, double-locking the door behind him. "I don't trust my workers," he moans in a whisper. "Huh! That lot would sell their souls to the Krauts for an extra ration of bread. Right, then, it seems you want to be a photo-engraver. You don't get to be one just like that, let me tell you. I teach at École Estienne. My pupils study for three years, after which there are three more years as an apprentice, and I can tell you that you don't know everything about photoengraving until you've been doing it for ten years. So if you've got sixteen years to spare, which would surprise me, you could perhaps become a pho-toengraver. And I did say perhaps."

"I don't want to be a professional photoengraver, I just want to... well, you know... learn a few little things, to make copies of rubber stamps for example."

"I've said I don't want to help anymore, it's too dangerous. Here the workers are watching, I'm sure of that. When I work at night there are sometimes traces left on the machines. And there are traitors everywhere. Which network are you with, Keller?"

"MLN."

"I was with the OCM,[1] but since they've gone over to the social-ists, I've joined the MLN. The socialists, huh... Why not work with the Jews, while we're at it!"

Did Goumard pretend to spit on the floor when he said 'Jews'? I think so. I'd just realized why Cachoud had taken the precaution of telling me to introduce myself as an agent of the MLN and not of the 6th section.

"Now it's over with, I don't help anyone any longer, as I've already said," he went on, without giving me time to respond.

"In that case, I'm sorry I've been wasting your time, M. Goumard. I'll leave now..."

He cut me off.

1. Organisation civile et militaire: Civil and Military Organization—one of the Resistance networks in the occupied (northern) zone of France. [MM]

"If I agree to help you, it's because René told me you were the one who found out how to deal with Waterman ink. Just fancy! There are quite a few of us who've been racking our brains to find the formula for removing it. Lactic acid! I've done a bit of chemistry myself, and still I didn't find it. You're a good one, you are, Keller. And we're not going to let those bastards turn our country into a German province!"

I felt like spitting in his face to let him know what I thought of him, turning on my heel and slamming the door, but I needed this training so badly I had no choice.

Fortunately my training with Goumard went more quickly than expected, and I must say I didn't regret that. I'd never imagined I could accumulate so much knowledge in so short a time, but I think it was Goumard's xenophobia and the nauseating way he went on and on that made me surpass even myself, so that I could manage without him as soon as possible. He had it in for everyone—the Jews, the English, the darkies but still the Krauts above all.

I remember one of our last conversations: "Racist, me? Huh! Certainly not. I like the Poles when they're in Poland, the Turks when they're in Turkey. And the Jews, if they could only manage to find a country, eh. As far away as possible."

I was amused to hear Goumard, without realizing it, speaking up for the idea of Zionism. Once I even brought up the question of homosexuals, wondering if Goumard could imagine a country far enough away for them.

"Huh! With the madmen!" he grunted.

No, really, I wasn't going to miss Goumard.

Once we'd met, Cachoud never left me a moment's peace. The

more I did, the more he demanded. He even went so far as to ask for some police ID cards. And, of course, I always said yes, ignoring my exhaustion and my health. Delivering was my sole obsession.

June 1944. It was three months since I'd last been out in broad daylight. Now that I'd set up my photoengraving studio in the room on the top floor of my boarding house, my only outings were to the Rue des Saints-Pères and back. If I saw summer arrive, it was through the skylight of the 6th section's laboratory. It was promising to be a hot summer. We were suffocating, all five of us crammed together under the attic roof in the toxic stench of the chemicals. So I wasn't unhappy that day to go out to meet Ernest, with whom I had a rendezvous. Filling my lungs with the air outside under a sun at its zenith and listening to the rustle of the wind in the trees in full leaf gave me a sense of freedom I hadn't had for a long time. Paris seemed to have come alive as if there was nothing wrong with the world. Girls rode past on bicycles, holding on to their hats to stop them flying away. I heard children's laughter from the corner of the street where a boys' class was coming along, two abreast, under the watchful eye of a master with an authoritarian finger.

If the passengers in the convertible speeding toward the horizon hadn't been wearing Nazi uniforms, you would have thought it was just an ordinary June day.

I hurried along toward Notre Dame, where Ernest would probably be waiting for me already. I was sure Cachoud would have another of his impossible requests, to be fulfilled immediately if not sooner, of course. I'd seen Ernest many times since our reunion in the Hôtel Montpensier. Furtive meetings, just time enough to exchange documents. No question of having a discussion; action was of the essence. But this time he didn't talk about forged papers.

"Follow me, I've something urgent to tell you," he said as soon as I arrived.

We went down to walk along the embankment of the Seine.

"That's it," he said, "the Jewish Legion is about to come into being. Just imagine, Adolphe, all the Jewish resistance movements fighting under the same flag. You, the EIF and the 6th section, us, the MJS and the AJ (Armée juive: Jewish Army). If we bring all our forces together, we'll pull more weight."

"But we're together already. We all work together."

"Yes, but this time we're amalgamating, showing that the Jewish Resistance is united. In the *maquis* there are men who are only waiting for the signal to regroup under the orders of the Jewish Legion."

The much-vaunted Jewish Legion. Ernest had been dreaming of it for ages. Since the beginning of the war he and many others had been thinking of an army that would bring together all the Jewish volunteers available and that, by its very existence alone, would cry out to the whole world that the Jews knew how to defend themselves, to fight and, above all, that they could win.

"I'm in contact with a London agent. Thanks to him we've already received some weapons," he went on, "and more are due to arrive. He wants me to draw up a list of the extent of our network, the number of combatants—we have to show that there are lots of us and that we have a solid structure. Give me the address of the lab and the names of those working there."

"Names and addresses—are you completely mad? I'm not giving the address of the lab nor the names of anyone at all."

"You've no confidence in us, is that it?"

"Confidence in you, yes. As long as you're not making lists. Who is this man who's provided weapons for you? What tells you it isn't a trap?"

"There's no trap, everything's safe. It's London that sent him. We've already gone through him and there's been no problems."

"What's he called?"

"Charles Porel. Make your own investigations if you like but do you really think Cachoud would trust just anyone?"

"Cachoud trusts him?"

"That's what I'm saying. So?"

"Don't count on me."

I saw Ernest's muscular body tense. In exasperation, he turned round and took a few steps. The wind made the skirts of his raincoat flap furiously and even from behind I could tell how angry he was. When he turned round to face me, the blue of his eyes had darkened intensely. He gave me a challenging look that would have made a whole army go pale. But I, who had not lowered my eyes before Brunner, was not going to flinch facing Ernest.

"You're a coward." He flung the words in my face. "You're afraid. Afraid of fighting." It was obvious that Ernest expected some reaction from me, but I gave nothing away, not one address, not one scrap of information, and I calmly held his icy glare until he turned on his heel and went off without saying goodbye. I watched him go. When his silhouette was nothing but a spot in the distance, I knew I'd lost one of my dearest friends.

I set off home with a lump in my throat. Had I been right? The problem with our relations with London was that everything was so difficult to verify. Who was talking to whom?

We never knew. If Cachoud was confident, however, it must mean the operation was secure. I was assailed by doubts, and when I got back, Otter didn't fail to notice that. I explained what the problem was.

"You said nothing, I hope?"

"No, nothing at all."

"Very good. I'll bring it up at the next meeting of the 6th, and we'll see what the others think."

"But what do you think about it?"

"The same as you. The laboratory above everything."

When Otter attended the meeting of the 6th section, he wasn't the only one to raise the matter. Those in charge had heard as well. Everyone was talking about the new supply channel for weapons for the Jewish Legion. But in the end the meeting decided that the 6th section wouldn't be part of it, even if it meant the others seeing us as something we weren't. Cowards.

The following month terrible news came from Drancy. The convoys were continuing, one after the other and more and more of them. The numbers were driving me crazy.

Summer hit me with its share of nasty surprises and sorrow.

Along with that, everything was happening in the lab the way I wouldn't have wanted. Photoengraving was giving me a lot of problems with all my makeshift equipment. There were botched pieces of work, and I had to go back to square one without losing my composure, without letting myself get discouraged. Sometimes I couldn't complete an order for lack of time, and the names at the bottom of the list had to be sacrificed. I couldn't bear that. I was so exhausted I was more and more worried about making mistakes from lack of concentration, and I was getting nervous, paranoiac. Outside I constantly thought I was being followed. I had a premonition something bad was going to happen. Before going to the 6th's laboratory, I would walk around the block several times to make sure that passer-by over there, or this one here wasn't a policeman or a spy. The secondhand bookseller always had a shifty look, the butcher and the baker as well. And that couple on the bench, hadn't he had a look at me before pretending to kiss his girlfriend? Assailed by doubt once again, I would change my route. Exhausting! As far as my health was concerned, my body was responding rather badly to the succession of sleepless nights and undernourishment. I was thin and weak and frequently fainted. But what worried me most of all was the condition of my right eye that had been running constantly for some time, during the night as well so that in the morning it took me more than half an hour to unstick my eyelids without tearing out the lashes. No time to go to the doctor, even though I was firmly convinced that my sight was getting worse and worse. Believe me, losing an eye is the worst thing that can happen to a forger.

In the last week of July Otter came rushing in bearing news that was to be a terrible blow for me. All the main people in charge of the MJS and the AJ, but also some of the Dutch network and the FTP-MOI as well, had just been arrested by the Gestapo. Cachoud and Ernest were among them. The arrests had taken place during a gathering organized by the so-called London agent who had been the cause of my disagreement with Ernest a month ago. My hunch had turned out to be correct! By sacrificing my friendship with Ernest, I had at least saved the 6th's laboratory. The man who had introduced himself to them as Charles Porel, claiming to belong to British Intelligence, was in reality a German, an Abwehr agent.[2] Our comrades had fallen into the trap and got nabbed when they arrived at the rendezvous. I simply couldn't believe it...

2. German counterintelligence. [MM]

It was a double disaster. On the one hand every branch of the OJC was affected, except the 6th. Could the organization still function shorn of its main leaders? Perhaps. We hoped so. In the *maquis* at least the fighters were continuing the struggle, and they were sufficiently well structured and autonomous to hold out. But for how long?

On the psychological level, the arrest of Ernest and, especially, that of Cachoud were devastating. I'd thought Cachoud was untouchable.

"Get out, the lot of you, go and hide!" Otter ordered with a catch in his voice that betrayed how distraught he was.

Since I thought he looked pale, I asked him, "You didn't give anyone the address of the lab?"

"No. You didn't either?"

"Of course not."

"You never know. We'd better wait three days, that's more sensible."

I quickly stuffed several rubber stamps, documents and chemicals in an attaché case, in the event I found the lab had been discovered when I came back. As for the photoengraving equipment at my boarding house, there was no point going to get it; indeed, it would be best not to set foot there again, since if I'd been followed, my cover there would obviously have been blown. As we left, Otter, who didn't seem to have told us everything, said solemnly, "That's not all. Cachoud died under torture."

Cachoud 'died under torture'.

We heard lots of details about their arrest. In Fresnes, as in all prisons, the walls had ears and our networks had sympathizers. I learned that they were all kicked and beaten but were also subjected to the ordeal of the bath. Cachoud was made the whipping boy and suffered the 'worst humiliations', to use the words in which it was reported to me. The details of the tortures he'd suffered stopped there, and it was up to my imagination to do the rest. 'Humiliation'. What unspeakable sufferings that word concealed!

We were told in precise detail how it happened. When the Gestapo handed over our comrades to the Abwehr, Cachoud was in such a bad state they wouldn't take him. In reality he was almost dead, he was no use to them. So the Gestapo took it upon themselves to finish him off, with the others looking on, by chucking him over the banisters. Cachoud hit the ground five floors below. That was the end of the matter for him, but it was going to take me a long time to get over it.

As for the others, they were now waiting their turn in Fresnes Prison, locked up in the block for those condemned to death. I continued to believe that, even under torture, none had talked nor would talk, and that the networks would not be broken up.

"Here, same time, in three days," we'd said before we parted. And it was better not to think of the consequences of the lab being inactive for three days if we didn't want to go back ravaged by a sense of guilt.

I had a few bucks left in my pocket, enough to find a hideout. I took refuge in a little hotel for students in Rue de l'Échaudé. I didn't have a suitcase, so in order not to arouse the receptionist's suspicions I took a room for one night only, intending to prolong my stay subsequently. On no account should I go back to the lab, but that didn't mean the network was broken. We had established a pretty simple technique for getting in contact. Every day at eleven in the morning one of our agents was at a crossroads in the district. On Mondays it was outside the Sorbonne, Tuesdays at Notre Dame, etc. If I didn't want the delivery of forged papers to be completely paralyzed for three days, it was imperative that I didn't miss the next day's rendezvous. No sooner had I settled into my new room than I drew the curtains and opened my precious attaché case. It contained the bare essentials: identity cards, demobilization certificates, ration cards, blank birth and baptismal certificates. Stamps and all colors of ink. That was enough to keep me going, even if at a slower pace.

The next day Penguin was waiting for me at the Sorbonne. He seemed relieved to see me. He'd been afraid I wouldn't turn up. We took the time to have a longer conversation. He was also deeply affected by the arrest of our men and was worried about my morale.

Since he was the one who'd recruited me and I was the youngest, he still had a fatherly, protective attitude toward me, as if he felt responsible, and even from a distance he tried to make sure that nothing happened to me. He gave a long sigh before starting to speak. "Listen, I know that the lab's going to be closed for a while, but if I haven't got the documents, I can't do anything. You know that I have two groups of thirty kids to take out during the week. We're in one hell of a fix."

"I've got the papers for you."

"What?"

"I've come to hand them over to you. I did them during the night."

"Unbelievable!"

We exchanged attaché cases and he left with the full one, I with the empty one.

At the same time three days later I climbed the stairs in Rue des Saints-Pères. No one had followed me from Rue de l'Échaudé.

When I opened the door, Suzie and Herta were already there, faithful to their post. The laboratory hadn't been found but there was lots of work to catch up on.

We'd just gotten back to work, when Otter burst into the room, his face whiter than ever: "They've got Penguin and the kids!"

At the same time, we learned that a group described as 'dangerous terrorists', specially sent there from the prisons, had arrived in Drancy and that Brunner had lost no time at all in locking them up in the basements of the camp, under maximum security.

The internees had been very moved to see them arrive, for the men were in rags and their emaciated faces bore the marks of torture. There were about thirty of them we were told. Who could these men Brunner called terrorists be? It didn't take us long to figure it out. From the descriptions they were our comrades, Ernest and all those who were with Cachoud when he'd been arrested.

"Why had they been sent to Drancy?"

It's easy to work that out. The allied armies were advancing on the capital, and the Nazis were in difficulty, so Brunner was being extra zealous. Rather than leaving their execution to the prison system, he wanted to see to it himself. If they were defeated, he wouldn't be going back to Germany empty-handed—he could give his Führer thirty of the most active members of the Jewish Resistance. My friends' tragic fate was sealed; they would be leaving for Pitchipoï with the next convoy.

"And Penguin?"

Penguin, as I later learned, was on a convoy for Auschwitz with the thirty children in his charge. Neither he nor the kids survived it.

5

SUMMER 1945. Almost a year since everyone took up their lives again from where they had broken off. But the war still wasn't yet over, and I was still a forger.

After the liberation of Paris a year before, I'd volunteered for the army as a stretcher-bearer in order to be in the combat zones. I wanted to continue to work in one way or another to help bring the war to an end, but unarmed.

The army's secret service was looking for a forger to allow their intelligence agents, parachuted behind enemy lines, to locate the less well-known concentration camps, notably those where medical experiments on human beings were carried out, before the Nazis could destroy all the evidence of their atrocities. Someone or other must have talked, my name have gotten around. One day two men came to see me in the barracks where I was stationed. One was Lieutenant Colonel Pommès-Barrère, head of the Centre de liaison et documentation (CLD) and the Direction générale des études et recherches (DGER) or, if you prefer, of the French army's counterespionage services. He was accompanied by Major Maillet, head of missions. I immediately took up my post in the DGER. Our department was attached to the Ministère des prisonniers de guerre et des déportés (MPGD),[1] the minister of which was a cold-eyed young soldier, scarcely thirty years old, by the name of François Mitterrand. From one day to the next I was promoted to the rank of second lieutenant and lodged in the Hôtel Doisy, close to the Place de l'Étoile, having a whole floor of the CLD at my disposal, and even a car and a driver, with all expenses taken care of by the army. I had become a state forger, a new status, perhaps even with career prospects. As the rules of the secret and intelligence services demanded, I had to work under a double identity, and I'd kept the one I'd had in the Resistance: Julien Adolphe Keller. For everyone else—family, friends, old colleagues from the 6th section—I passed myself off as a clerk, a common ministry pen pusher.

For a year, until the capitulation of the Axis forces and the liberation of the camps, I made German papers. No sooner had I arrived than I was given models of German travel warrants, train tickets, identity cards, passports, military ID. I also had to make papers for foreign workers in Germany to allow intelligence agents who couldn't speak German to pass for STO volunteers. Given the urgency and the quantity of forged papers to produce, I was obviously soon under pressure. The work was as delicate as ever, and it was imperative that the forged documents were undetectable. Never having had to make German identity cards before, I was faced with characteristics that were new to me. They had both transparent and opaque watermarks. The rigidity of the paper, the weight and the coloring techniques were all different. Of course I had more technical means at my disposal—I could buy high-performance equipment—but I still had to carry

1. Center of Liaison and Documentation; General Directorate for Study and Research; Ministry of Prisoners of War and Deportees. [MM]

out a large number of experiments and apply my ingenuity.

I recovered all my equipment from the 6th section laboratory and from my former boarding house in Rue Jacob. In separate rooms on my floor in Hôtel Doisy I'd installed a darkroom, a photoengraving studio, a print room, an office for filling out documents, a room for coloring and deleting, one for making paper and another in which my old Singer sewing machine stood in pride of place; it was the one my father had used to make his customers' suits and that I used to cut out revenue stamps. I printed them directly on gummed paper and, to make the perforations, I'd replaced the sewing needle with a needle from a syringe that matched the size of the holes exactly.

On this particular morning it's barely five o'clock when the first rays of the sun appear in my room in Hôtel Doisy. Through the window I have a view of a colorless sky with a strange, thin, slightly frayed cloud. I put on my coat and hurry out. The six new intelligence agents arrived during the night. I'm going to have a lot to do in the next few days.

My driver, who waits for me outside the hotel every morning, takes me to the DGER and parks outside the apartment block. Major Maillet is there to greet me and opens the door of the building. With his square jaw and short black hair parted on the side, he looks like an American film actor. His work for the DGER is to train the agents in military espionage before sending them out into enemy territory. Both physical and mental training. Apart from him—he sleeps there—the premises of the CLD, a building with four vast stories composed of little offices either side of a long corridor, are completely empty at this early hour. My floor is right at the top. It's entirely at my disposal apart from the space behind a door that's always kept locked and to which Maillet alone has the key. I go up the stairs with Maillet and follow him through that door. This part is laid out like a large apartment with bedrooms, kitchen and shower-room. No one besides Maillet and myself is authorized to go in there or to make contact with the occupants.

The intelligence agents, accustomed to sleeping with one eye open, appear in the doorways of their bedrooms. Maillet introduces them to me one by one. Six strapping young guys, muscular and well-nourished, scrupulously selected from among the best agents of the army, who've just completed two months of arduous military training in a house in the suburbs, the location of which is kept secret. They're going to be sent to Germany in two groups of three, each group consisting of a leader to supervise operations, a radio operator and an infiltration agent.

For a parachute operation to be successful, each member of the group has to be provided with all the proofs of his existence in the country. Identity documents, travel permits, rent receipts, library card, sales slip from a store, bus or cinema ticket, railway ticket from such and such a town on such and such a date, prescription for his asthma, an old crumpled letter from his mother or fiancée, with a stamp canceled by the post office.

Everything a man might carry with him and which, should he be caught, might save his life. And of course that means that each document has to be produced individually and that nothing must be left to chance. I have a week to invent a credible new past for each of them and create the proofs, always making sure their cover is easy for them to assimilate, mixing in a little truth with the false or starting out from their real life history to construct a new one. It's essential to spend hours and hours talking to them before going on to make the documents. That day I'm lucky. Two of the men are from Alsace, speak fluent German and even know the areas where they're going to be parachuted in. It's more complicated for the others because we have to start entirely from scratch.

The meetings and conversations go on one after the other without pause throughout this long and exhausting day. It's like this every time new agents pass through the CLD before taking the plunge. There's so much to do you don't notice time, you forget to eat. By the time I leave, night's already falling and everyone's gone home. A special meeting's been arranged for this evening, and I have to hurry to get there. It's a reunion with all my former comrades in the Resistance. So far my work's left me so little spare time that I haven't seen most of them.

There's lots of us there that evening, a good thirty in that cheap little cafeteria on Rue Claude-Bernard. All those from the 6th section laboratory are there: Giraffe, Ackerberg, Heron, Otter, Water Lily, Suzie, Herta and René Polski, Cachoud's assistant. It's good to see everyone again. Water Lily greets me warmly, gives me a glass of wine and talks about chemistry, which she's decided to study. We chat for a moment when suddenly, in the middle of the general hubbub, there's a laugh I recognize, a very familiar one, coming from the back of the room. I survey the room, and what do I see? A young man, tall, blond, pipe in his mouth and a steely look. No need for introductions, it's Ernest Appenzeller accompanied by Henri Phohorylès and Jacques Lazarus, all three of whom were in Brunner's last convoy! I couldn't understand it. My first reaction was to wonder whether the wine had been spiked. It's crazy, I think I'm seeing ghosts! Am I seeing things? Going mad? Is it the emotion or perhaps the post-traumatic shock everyone's talking about? And the others, can they see them as well? There's no one in the restaurant who looks surprised; everyone's laughing, drinking, smoking and talking their heads off. I push my way through to them and, with a couple of roars of laughter and pats on the back, they tell me how they escaped. They had a few implements and with them they managed to saw through the bars over the window of the railroad car. And since the train, constantly halted by the sabotage of the Resistance, had only reached Saint-Quentin after four days, several of them escaped by night and got back to the capital with just a few minor injuries and empty stomachs. I haven't seen Ernest since the day I refused to give him the address of the laboratory, but that matter is closed. He, who had so often come close to death, has once again escaped from Brunner's claws. He's alive, that's the main thing. And, as you will see later on, Ernest and I were going to have a few missions to carry out together, in a different struggle.

But let's leave Ernest and concentrate for a moment on Pierre Mouchenik, called 'Pierrot', who I met for the first time at that party. Pierrot, twenty-five, was a former member of the Jewish Army who, after Maurice Cachoud left, had taken charge of the production of forged papers in Nice. The distance between Paris and Nice meant that during the war we couldn't meet, but we had often corresponded in invisible ink. He was blond with blue eyes, a man who always seemed at ease. He had a gift for language, an enthusiasm that you got caught up in and, above all, that particular way of speaking to a crowd, looking each person in the eye so that everyone felt it concerned them personally. He was a virtuoso in the art of taking a breath and pausing, knew how to hold the suspense or to indulge in repartee. He always had a joke up his sleeve, an anecdote or a story that sounded like a novel. And his charm had a devastating effect on women. But, above all, he had a strong belief in liberty and equality. I took a liking to him from the moment he opened his lips. He was the one who came over to me and insisted I tell him what I'd been doing since the Liberation. Obviously I gave him the official version of my activities: lieutenant in the army. He seemed disappointed I wasn't available, and it wasn't long before I knew why.

One week later the DGER was jumping for joy. We'd just heard that the Axis forces had capitulated. The missions of the agents we were keeping hidden were canceled, and my fabrication of German papers stopped abruptly. I was starting to destroy the documents when my boss, Colonel Pommès-Barrière, came to discuss a new urgent assignment with me. It wasn't about forged papers anymore but a laborious cartographical task mapping Indo-China with a view to a potential recapture by the forces of the French administration of the colony. I complied without objection, an order was an order. But as the maps piled up beneath the lens of my reproduction camera, I was beset by a profound sense of inner conflict. I no longer felt I was in the right place. Military espionage in times of peace was no concern of mine, and I found the prospect of taking part in the colonial war that was on the horizon sickening, terrifying even. I'd never made a decision to be a forger. A soldier even less. What I'd done in the past I'd done because I had to; I'd had no choice. I knew that after the maps they were going to ask me to make forged documents for a war that had no justification in my eyes and that, like all wars, would have innocent victims. I wouldn't be able to obey the orders that would come, not because I didn't like them, but because my principles forbade it: if the insurrection of the

Indo-Chinese was to take place, shouldn't I see it as comparable to what the Resistance had been for the French?

The word didn't exist at the time, but I was deeply anti-colonialist. The next day I decided, despite the insistence of my superiors, who wanted to keep me, to resign. No sooner had Pierrot heard of this than he had people looking for me everywhere. It was Otter who found me several weeks later. I was living like a destitute in a tiny hovel on Rue de Charenton, with no water or electricity, trying to rebuild my life by getting enough little photographic commissions to keep me going.

I saw Pierrot once, then again and again. Each time he was very excited, more and more impatient, a real live wire...

When Pierrot appealed to me and explained that the aim of his group's activities was to allow the survivors of the camps to immigrate into Palestine illegally, I at first refused. It was no use him using every possible argument and telling me that it was a matter of the future of several hundred thousand people, I remained adamant. I refused to start taking part in illegal activities again now the war was over.

"What made you change your mind?"

To convince me, Pierrot arranged for me to go with some GIs to the refugee camps in Germany. It was January 1946. There were four of us in the jeep. We'd crossed the German frontier an hour ago when one of them pointed to a an immense brick camp in the distance behind which was a collection of low, rectangular huts set in the middle of a muddy-looking field.

Suddenly I saw them, on the other side of the barbed wire in prisoners' striped costumes. There were hundreds coming slowly towards us with questioning looks. I'd known what to expect when I'd agreed to come on this trip, and I'd prepared myself for it but, faced with this throng of black-and-white costumes that amassed along the barbed wire in a few minutes, I caught myself thinking for a moment that I'd rather not get out of the jeep.

I managed to talk to one of them who spoke fluent French. He was Polish, a former French teacher. He told me he'd have to be dead before he'd set foot in his old country again. They all said the same. The governments of their countries had betrayed them, being on European soil would always remind them of the atrocities they'd been subjected to. Nothing could break their determination, even if it meant staying in these camps to wait, or rot, for years if need be, until they could finally obtain a visa for Palestine. A certain solidarity had been established there. Families had been recreated—children had been born, adults had adopted children that weren't theirs—which nothing apart from death could break up, the Pole said with a tender look at a woman sitting some way away with her baby, who I realized had become his new family.

What most shocked me during that short trip was to find, on the way back, hordes of savage children prowling around near the camps.

When we set off, it had been agreed that the GIs would take me to see several camps for displaced persons in the area, but one had been enough for me, and I asked to be taken straight back to Paris. Suddenly, as we rounded a bend, in the distance I saw slim silhouettes standing right in the middle of the road. There were at least fifteen of them, and their intention seemed to be to block our way. As we approached I realized, in the light of the headlamps, that they were children armed with sticks. They were no more than fourteen years old, some even very small, six or seven perhaps. The driver switched off the lights, slowed down but didn't stop. I didn't immediately understand why the GIs took out their guns and aimed them at the kids, who immediately drew back to the side, though without showing the least sign of fear. They left just a very narrow gap for us to pass through, and while I was looking at them, one hit my window violently with his fist uttering incomprehensible cries of abuse. To see such hatred and rage on a child's face was so frightening it made my blood run cold. Even at the risk of injuring some of them, the driver had no choice but to accelerate to get the jeep free since it was once more surrounded. No sooner had we passed them than the children regrouped and attacked us from behind, throwing sticks and stones as the jeep disappeared into the darkness.

One of the GIs explained that they were children who'd survived the concentration camps, from which they'd been liberated, and now roamed around them organized in outlaw gangs, attacking farms and houses to find food and terrorizing the local population. Their parents were dead, exterminated by the Nazis and, left to themselves, they showed extreme violence toward adults whom they looked on as their enemies. The road we were driving along passed close to a camp of refugee orphans. They'd been sent there in their thousands, by force. When the liberators arrived, most were found surrounded by corpses; for months they'd had to fend for themselves to survive, and they didn't trust anyone anymore. As we continued on our way, for twenty, thirty, forty kilometers we saw other gangs taking off across the ditches as the jeep passed.

That trip brought back to me the shock of the Liberation. It was only when the occupying force had been driven out of the country that I experienced my first great disillusionment. I'd dreamed of victory—it was a hope I'd clung on to with all my might, and I'd been naïve enough to imagine it would bring in its wake the end of groups being despised, the end of racism. I was perplexed and horrified at the number of refugees no one had any idea what to do with. Palestine was still under the British mandate, and the White Paper was in force, restricting emigration there to a trickle while there were record numbers of visa applications, hundreds of thousands. The situation was dragging on and on.

Everything was deadlocked.

I felt strong empathy with these survivors of the concentration camps that no one wanted anything to do with, these children who didn't believe in anything any longer and whose faith in the world needed to be restored, these men and women who longed for some far-off land where they could rebuild their lives, shielded from persecution. For once they wanted to be masters of their own fate. They wanted to emigrate to Palestine. Where they went was a matter of indifference to me—I wasn't a Zionist—but I was strongly in favor of the idea that every individual, especially if they were persecuted and their life in danger, should have the right to move freely, to cross borders, to choose where their exile should take them.

No sooner had I gotten back to Paris than I picked up the phone and dialed Pierrot who, as I was well aware, was itching for me to call.

6

IT'S LONG BEEN PITCH DARK. It's October 1947 now. I've covered the windows with heavy-duty black paper to keep me out of sight of inquisitive neighbors, so they don't start wondering about the light that's almost never off. Prudence is ever my watchword.

Ernest's order had been ready for ages: passport, driver's license and courier's ID for him and two of his men. On the other hand, I know I'm unlikely to be satisfied with the result of a collective Brazilian visa demanded by a 'Monsieur Pol', the broad rubber stamp that has to be used to get three hundred applicants for the journey to Palestine to the port. I have a problem with the one they've given me as a model. The letters are too flattened on one side and the ink runs, leaving blots. Is it that the original has traps, deliberate design faults? Should I rectify them or not at all? If at least I had two different models, as I always insist on, I'd be able to compare them and know where to make a few corrections. After a long analysis by microscope, I have no choice but to proceed from experience. I decide to reduce the blots, though without removing them entirely, but to hardly correct the squashed letters at all. I make a negative of the model, then a relief photoengraving that I mold in rubber by heating in order to obtain a negative proof of the stamp. In general, I heat the ordinary stamps by using a vulcanizer—available in stores, which is used to repair bicycle inner tubes—but in this case, for a much larger visa stamp, I resort to my good old method: the clothes iron. I always have the most recent models without, for all that, ever having ironed anything. I've just acquired one of the first electric irons designed for household use. It doesn't have a thermostat, but I'm so accustomed to using them that I just have to hold the iron a few centimeters away from my face to be able to estimate the temperature more or less to the last degree. As it cools, the negative stamp hardens, allowing me to make the positive. Then I go on to analyze the ink of the original before mixing my colors to achieve an exact replica, a vermilion red. As far as the precise tint is concerned, I don't have any particular difficulty but, after verification by artificial light, by infrared and ultraviolet rays, I discover two traps that are set to identify forgeries: the ink contains a substance that adds extra brilliance and a phosphorescent substance that doesn't show up in the ultraviolet rays. As far as the brilliance is concerned, I fortunately have the experience of my work for the Resistance and the DGER—I know I'll be able to reproduce it by adding some gum arabic, but I still need to do a few trials to find the right amount. As for the phosphorescence of the ink, there are some kinds that are revealed or not according to the speed of the light and there again, I have to seek, think and test.

Some hours later, I can finally check the result and compare the two stamps. I've reduced the blots and the flattened letters nicely, but I'm just not satisfied with my forged rubber stamp. Now it's too sharp, too perfect compared with the original to be real. If in doubt, it's best to start all over again.

"Who exactly are you working for?"

From then on I was working for the Aliyah Bet,[1] the clandestine network for the immigration of concentration camp survivors to Palestine. I was working with most of those who had made up the Nice network, who now formed the French branch of the Haganah,[2] and, as always, they expected me to perform miracles, more miracles than could be demanded of a single man.

When I got back from Germany, Pierre introduced me—in a town house on Avenue Kléber that looked like the embassy of a clandestine government—to Abraham Polonski, the man called 'M. Pol', the creator of the Jewish Army, to which all those of the South Zone group had taken the oath. He was short but impressive with his broad shoulders and leader's air. Commanding troops came naturally to him, and his authority as a war leader had brought him the nickname 'Little Napoleon'.

There were serious political differences at the heart of the organization, but since we were all pursuing the same goal, we were able to put our disagreements to one side in order to combine our forces. Nevertheless, like me, my closest friends tended to follow the prewar Russian line: Marxist, defending the idea of collective labor and of the kibbutz. We each had our personal motivation for taking part in this illegal immigration. For Pierrot, for example, it was the future of the young people that was most important. He wanted to help them reintegrate into society. His work therefore included the creation of school farms for adolescents and bringing together families that had been broken up. There was always a social side to his activities that was to become his vocation later on. Others, like

1. "Aliyah", a Hebrew word for the immigration of Jews to the Holy Land. Bet, the letter "B" of the Hebrew alphabet, expresses the clandestine nature of the organization of the immigration.

2. Haganah (Hebrew: defense) was the Zionist military organization that eventually became the national army of Israel. [MM]

M. Pol and his adjutant were following the idea of the creation of a national home for the Jews in Palestine, as stipulated by the Balfour Declaration,[3] a dream all Zionists clung to. Then there were those for whom helping the survivors to go to Palestine was the logical continuation of the Resistance. They had taken the oath to the Jewish Army. The great majority wanted to go and live there as soon as a political solution made it possible. But as far as I was concerned, it was above all the free movement of people of all nations that was at stake, perhaps because of my childhood, or something I'd inherited from my family, the years of forced exile my parents had had to endure. And then I had this painful memory of our first attempt to immigrate to France. I was only five at the time. After spending a month on the ship that took us from Buenos Aires to Marseilles, we were expelled only a few days after our arrival and forced to take refuge in Turkey, where we hoped to obtain permits. It was a long wait, two years during which we had to survive in abject poverty. And the birth of my little sister put a new obstacle in the way of our application. Since she hadn't been born in Argentina, the Argentine government refused to grant her nationality. As for the Turkish authorities, they objected to her naturalization because she hadn't been 'conceived' in Turkey. She was in a legal vacuum, and that prevented us from returning to France. It was then that I really understood the signification of the word 'papers', those indispensable documents that allow you to move legally from one state to another, the acquisition of which, for a family like mine that had spent decades wandering from one exile to another, proved particularly complicated. If I'm making a point of telling you stories from my

3. On November 2nd, 1917 British Foreign Secretary Arthur James Balfour declared "sympathy with Jewish Zionist aspirations" and wrote to the Zionist representatives: "His Majesty's Government view with favour the establishment in Palestine of a national home for the Jewish people, and will use their best endeavors to facilitate the achievement of this object, it being clearly understood that nothing shall be done which may prejudice the civil and religious rights of existing non-Jewish communities in Palestine or the rights and political status enjoyed by Jews in any other country." [MM]

childhood, it's because it was there, in Turkey, that I became aware of two fundamental things that governed and conditioned most of the acts of resistance in my life. The first is the power of money and the injustices it causes, and the second is that without papers one is condemned to immobility.

Let's go back to where we left off. From now on my contacts in the Haganah were M. Pol, his assistant, Pierrot, or Ernest, who, as always, dealt with dangerous missions. The mission for most of the agents in the network was to coordinate operations from escaping from the camps to embarking at the ports. The camps were in Germany, Austria and Poland. You don't empty a camp in one go. They had to get the displaced persons out in groups of thirty, in covered trucks, taking a few from each camp until they had a total of five hundred survivors per boat. The Aliyah units were secretly infiltrated into the camps and worked together with the Service d'évacuation et de regroupement des enfants et familles (SERE),[4] a state-registered organization that gave us official government cover.

I had to provide forged collective visas for the escapees. A single tourist visa could be used for thirty to fifty people, sometimes even a hundred depending on circumstances. The nationality of the papers depended on the language spoken by the group of survivors. And the names on the lists I made for the visa were invented, totally fictitious. Every person in the group was informed of their false name at the last moment, immediately before they left. It was very complicated. The White Paper still forbade any immigration at all, and it was absolutely essential that our groups should not arouse the suspicions of the British intelligence service, which was why the movements of the immigrants should take the form of children's summer camps or tours for groups of adults. The final destination

4 Evacuation and reunification service for children and families.

never appeared on the documents. And since the convoys would have been systematically detected if everyone came from the same place, I also had to make a pile of papers supporting a fictitious place of origin, such as train tickets or customs stamps from different countries.

I had also to provide forged documents for all the couriers and those who organized the escapes, who went all over Europe. For them I made something of everything: driving licenses, passports, visas, for they drove the refugees in trucks and had to cross borders. And of course there were also the members of the crews of the ships, not to mention the authorizations for mooring in the ports where they took on their human cargo. In most cases the passengers were officially embarking for a Latin American country, and it was only once they were out at sea that they changed course and headed for the coast of Palestine. But I knew that very few of the boats reached the right port. As soon as they entered British territorial waters off Palestine, British warships barred their way and escorted them to Cyprus, where the illegal immigrants were once more placed in camps for displaced persons, waiting for visas that never came. But even Cyprus was better than nothing: it wasn't Germany or Poland, and the concentration camp survivors were closer to their hoped-for destination.

On joining the organization I was very quickly handicapped by the insecure conditions where I was living in Rue Charenton. They provided me with new premises—2, Rue d'Écosse, near the Panthéon—in which I immediately installed all my equipment, the same as I'd had for the 6th section and the secret service, improved by a few items I'd recovered from old laboratories of the Resistance. Now I had a large, clean room at my disposal with running water, gas and electricity. There was a financial section through which one could get access to funds to meet urgent situations, I don't know exactly how, it wasn't my business. I've always hated dealing with money. All I know is that Pierrot had set up two export-import firms, bogus companies that allowed the organization to pay me a small salary to compensate me for my expenses, but also so that I could eat in cheap cafeterias, for I was the only one who didn't get a ration card.

However unlikely it may seem to you, after everything I'd done, especially for the army, I was underground again, therefore paid in cash and my name didn't appear on any official register. After I left the secret service I had, however, set about trying to obtain my papers. All that I had was an out-of-date army ID card and a receipt from the prefecture with 'Jew' stamped diagonally across it. The police weren't used to seeing that type of document any more. The Liberation had been over for a year, and everyone had gotten their personal situation sorted out ages ago. Not me. The inspector who interviewed me thought I was a suspicious character. "Illegal," he said, "unless you can't show us your Argentine papers by the end of the month." I did finally manage to get my Argentine papers, but for a residence permit I had to provide proof of permanent employment, which I didn't have. My papers were stamped by the section in charge of deportation, and I had to come back within two weeks with all the proofs and documents required, otherwise I'd be on a ship back to Argentina.

That simple prefecture stamp sent me back to all the complicated paperwork my parents had had to submit to the authorities regularly to renew our residence permits when I was a child, with the constant fear of being expelled again and having to go into exile once more. At the time, I'd found all these supporting documents exhausting, all the proofs, the requests for extensions. But this time I took the threat of expulsion as a humiliation. I was indignant that the administration would have the power to throw me out when I'd worked for the Liberation and the reputation of a country where I believed I belonged.

Also, when I joined the Aliyah Bet, the first document I forged was for myself; as it had been when I'd joined the 6th section and the DGER, it was a kind of ritual. To return to my work as a forger hadn't been an easy decision. I remembered my first forgery. At that time there was no question that my activity was morally justified. We had to break the law. But did that mean I'd tumbled irredeemably into illegality? I'd always made sure that my knowledge and technical skill were solely used in the service of legitimate causes. I'd always made sure I never compromised with my sense of ethics, of morality. But once more I was outside the law, and I wondered whether, from the day I'd done my first forgery, I hadn't been caught up in a spiral I'd have difficulty getting out of my whole life through.

That morning Ernest arrived at the laboratory to collect his papers lugging an enormous suitcase and a large canvas bag containing weapons. A machine gun, a Sten submachine gun, a revolver, a large quantity of cartridges, clips for the Sten, plastic and detonators that he wanted me to keep until they were needed. Needed for what? I never found out. Ernest had retained his arrogance from the war years. His work was always terribly efficient, and no one could doubt his extreme loyalty, but he remained unpredictable.

Impossible to know what he was cooking up, and he always seemed to be preparing several things at the same time. The two of us had gotten into the habit of never asking each other questions about our respective missions. I didn't protest about the suitcase. I hadn't had a wink of sleep during the night and, just having managed to solve the thorny problem of the Brazilian visa, I was in a hurry to get some breakfast before going to deliver it to M. Pol.

We went to a café for a quick bite, and he accompanied me to the Haganah offices. M. Pol saw us separately and gave each of us new instructions. I left with a Madagascar visa, documents for a captain and boarding passes for the next day. No time for a rest. And it had been like that since the failure of the *Exodus*.

The *Exodus* was an attempt, organized by the Haganah for the Alyah Bet, to break the blockade. It was an American ship transporting survivors of the concentration camps, not in their hundreds but, for the first time, in their thousands. A record number of five thousand had arrived clandestinely in France and embarked at Port-de-Bouc in the south, determined to force a way through the blockade at all cost and not to accept being diverted to Cyprus.

When we heard that *Exodus* had failed and that the passengers were going to be brought back by force in British prison ships to their point of departure, all the members of the organization accompanied by numerous sympathizers hurried off to the quiet little village of Port-de-Bouc. I was one of them.

It was a scorching summer. It was hot and dry. The town, suddenly flooded with people, was in slow motion. We filled the beaches and the narrow streets, meeting friends and EIF comrades at every crossroads. We were watching for the ships to appear in the distance. The port was besieged by journalists. By the police as well. We were all waiting. The days passed, always the same. The beach, demonstrations, taking a stroll, then starting all over again. Almost a vacation compared with the solitude and darkness of my laboratory. All my friends were there. It was by watching them, as at ease in the water as on the sand, athletic bodies, suntanned, that I became aware of how different I was. At twenty-one I couldn't even swim, and I hadn't seen the sea since a summer camp at Berck-Plage—when I was eight. Fly a plane, on the other hand, I could do that, I'd been trained as a pilot by the Haganah. Copy any document perfectly, make explosives, find a solution to any technical difficulty, I could do that too, but seeing them enjoying themselves, I realized that I'd been deprived of life for four years.

On the beach, in the café, at the hotel, we talked everywhere and all the time about the future state, and we wanted it to be created in the image of the fraternity we could see in Port-Bouc; we would be the ones who built it, we'd make it a model of liberty and equality, and already we couldn't wait to get there. Until then, Zionist ideology hadn't meant anything to me, but I'd gradually come to believe in the possibility of a state where Jews could live without being persecuted; if they were always being thrown out of wherever they were, perhaps they needed somewhere else where they'd legitimately belong, where the law and public opinion would protect every individual without distinction of race, country of origin, nationality or faith. This country had to be built, even if it was only to heal the wounds of hundreds of years of persecution. We all wanted to believe that the *Exodus* would be our last fight before victory. This event had sown diplomatic discord between Britain and France, which was refusing to compel the would-be emigrants to disembark. They must have been very unhappy in London. In the displaced-persons camps throughout Europe a hundred and forty thousand survivors had started a hunger strike in solidarity, making headlines in the press, and at last public opinion seemed sympathetic to our cause. I was confident. Britain would end up giving way.

With our comrades we were on the alert. We were strong, we would stand together. We could make history. Together we were going to create something that would last—it was exhilarating, thrilling. Yes, there certainly was something historic happening there.

But at the end of a week we had to face facts. Nothing was happening. The situation could go on for a long time while there were still a number of ships to send on their way. The time on the beach with its great hopes was over. The new directive from the organization was as follows: work with the Aliyah Bet by doubling the number of ships, giving priority to those who had been through this ordeal. For me that meant twice as much work. For the organization the idea was to fill the camps in Cyprus to overflowing, thus continuing to destabilize London.

The only respite I allowed myself was to go to the reunions organized by Jacques Lazarus, whom people called Captain Jacquel. That particular evening there was a dinner at his house, and Ernest suggested we go together. Lazarus was a former professional soldier who, after having been discharged by Pétain, had created a *maquis* unit then, later on, the Jewish Combat Organization. He, like Ernest, was one of those who'd escaped from the last convoy. I didn't particularly feel like a 'war veteran', but I enjoyed going to these events to see my old pals. Most of them were helping the illegal immigration in one way or another and were aware of my work for the Haganah.

Ernest came to fetch me by car that evening. He was accompanied, as too often, by Isidore, another member of the network, which tended to get on my nerves. How many times had I told Ernest that no one besides Pierrot and himself should know the address of the lab? Ernest did just as he pleased. The weapons that morning, and now his companion this evening—it was too much for a single day. I flew into one of my fits of rage that had earned me the reputation of being bad tempered. But Ernest put my mind at rest by assuring me he would come to collect his 'gear' in the next few days.

Almost everyone had accepted Lazarus' invitation. Etty, Giraffe's sister, was a former member of the 6th, a woman with tremendous drive who belonged to a very active Marxist group. That evening she continually tried to speak to me alone. As soon as Ernest, Pierrot or Isidore came over she would slip away to another room in the apartment. Eventually, just as I was getting ready to leave, she put on her coat and threaded her way through the guests to go down the stairs with me.

"What you're doing's great," she said as we walked home together. "But would you agree to help those who're really fighting against the British?"

"Who're you talking about?"

"The Stern group," she replied in a whisper.

I'd heard of what the British usually called the Stern gang, a group that had no hesitation in organizing attacks on the British army and police. The members wanted to liberate the country and combined their extreme nationalism with a 'social-revolutionary' ideology. For them the Arabs in Palestine weren't the enemy, quite the contrary, they looked on them as potential allies in the struggle against the British imperialist yoke. The problem was that the Stern group's terrorist activities were strongly condemned by the Haganah, which worked in the diplomatic field, negotiating with Britain and, moreover, didn't hesitate to hand Stern group terrorists over to the British, who hanged them. That was why Etty kept quiet when members of the Haganah were around.

She walked home with me and wouldn't let me go in until I'd at least agreed to meet the leaders of the group in France.

A few days later, during a meeting of four members of the

French Stern group, Etty introduced me to Tibor Rosenberger, called 'Voltaire', a former member of the Hungarian resistance. He was a tall, elegant man, cultured and charismatic, with a passion for classical music and literature. He explained to me that there were various tendencies within the Stern group and that he totally disagreed with the extremists.

However, he was disgusted with the Haganah fighting the British while at the same time assisting them and handing over members of the group to them. He explained his own stance: the idea was to push the British out by, let's say, expeditious methods such as assassinations and ambushes. The majority of members of the Stern group were wanted by the police and needed forged papers to be able to move freely and avoid being hanged. But that wasn't all. Tibor also needed forged papers to organize the illegal immigration of former members of the Hungarian resistance he was close to. What appealed to me most in what he said was the existence of a Judeo-Arab faction in Palestine. My ideal, like Tibor's, was a Jewish-Arab state liberated from the British. After having talked together for hours and hours, we became friends, but terrorism remained our one point of disagreement. Added to that, there were risks in working for the Haganah and the Stern group at the same time for, even though they were pursuing the same goal, they were nonetheless at war with each other. But whatever they might have done, the lives of the wanted members of the Stern group were in danger, the British didn't treat them with kid gloves. None of those who'd been caught had escaped the gallows. I agreed to set up a laboratory for him and to deal with urgent requests until they found another forger. In fact, I already had someone in mind, a person who wouldn't need training and who I started looking for at once...

Suzie was still at the same address, continuing her studies at the Beaux-Arts. I had no problem finding her and invited her to dinner. I remember her foot tapping the floor under the table and her shining eyes when I explained that I couldn't work for both sides at the same time, that it was absolutely impossible for me to divide my working time in two and that if anyone in my network, Ernest or M. Pol, should hear of my double membership, it would be a disaster for the Stern agents.

She cut me short, not even giving me time to put in my request, "I want to work for the Stern group!"

From that day on I started my day in the Stern group's lab on Rue Clerc, in order to go through the problems Suzie had come up against, then hurried on to Rue d'Écosse, all the time taking thousands of precautions to make sure I wasn't being followed.

Everything worked perfectly. I'd found a way of helping both sides without betrayal. That was until the day when the Stern group asked me to make a delayed-action clockwork mechanism, when I'd always been firmly opposed to taking part in acts of terrorism. I have to explain that in all the networks I worked for I was not only the forger, but also the technical specialist. Whether it was devising cases or bags with false bottoms or making films or photographing archives, anything that involved technical problems was my province. By means of some roundabout questioning, I worked out that they were preparing to assassinate the British Foreign Minister, Ernest Bevin, who was firmly opposed to British troops being withdrawn from Palestine and was generally seen as the main defender of the White Paper. On top of that he was said to have made outrageously anti-Semitic remarks.

This business seriously troubled my conscience. I didn't want to be party to the assassination of anyone at all. How could I have looked at myself in the mirror if I felt personally responsible for the death of a man, even if he were an enemy? But if I refused, someone else would take it on, of that I was sure.

"So what did you say?"

I agreed to do it. I made the clock that would set off the detonators of the bomb that would blow Bevin to pieces. A man called Avner was going to go off to England with the contraption and place it in the spot where the assassination was to happen. I'd met Avner some time previously, in the Rue Clerc laboratory. He was the Stern group's man for dangerous missions. Their very own 'Ernest'. He'd recently arrived from Palestine on a very badly forged passport that had led to a lengthy interrogation that he'd just managed to survive. He couldn't take such a risk again and needed an impeccable passport. Avner told me that in the area where his kibbutz was, the kibbutzim lived in perfect harmony with the Bedouin villages around and that any conflicts that occurred were settled by delegates of the villages and the kibbutz, each showing great respect for the other. I loved that image. It confirmed me in my desire to go to that distant country, so full of promise. When, much later, I saw Avner again, he confessed to me, not without sadness, that the Israeli war of independence had finally driven the Bedouin out of the area.

Avner left with the package, carried out his mission and returned to Palestine.

We were supposed to hear of the death of Bevin through the newspapers. But a week later there was no word of it in them, and Bevin, very much alive, was attending a meeting of the cabinet. For a long time Avner must have wondered why the bomb hadn't exploded and, should he read these pages, he'll learn that the delayed-action mechanism I'd made was designed so it would never go off and, if it should, the plastic had been replaced by putty. An enemy or not, I had saved a life. No one ever spoke to me about the failure of the bomb. Today I couldn't care less if they could have thought me capable of such an act. Purely from the point of view of strategy, the assassination was really not a good idea, bearing in mind future negotiations. Anyway, we'd almost won the diplomatic battle. From the outset the United Nations had to decide between two proposals: two states, one Jewish, one Arabic, or a single, dual state. In either case Britain had been defeated and had to retire. Personally I was in favor of the second proposal, a mixed state, imagining its secular nature would cement peaceful coexistence, to my mind the only way of guaranteeing that everyone could practice their religion without one or the other dictating the laws. Utopian, you say? True, but that's what I've always been and still am. The UN finally came out in favor of two separate states, a decision that was to come into effect on May 14, 1948, a date that is familiar to many people. In the meantime Great Britain retained the mandate over the territory but her troops had to withdraw as soon as the states were set up. It wasn't exactly what I was hoping for, but it was a kind of victory.

In conformity with the United Nations' resolution, on May 14, 1948 David Ben-Gurion proclaimed the establishment of the state of Israel according to the agreed division of territory. The following day Egypt, Jordan and Lebanon attacked the nation that had just been born. It was at that time that the majority of my buddies in the organization emigrated to Palestine to help build the country. I had to make forged passports and visas for all my friends, and I watched as their photos marched past into the envelopes for M. Pol. When I saw Ernest's photo, I knew that he wouldn't be coming to pick up the weaponry he'd left with me. As for myself, I was to join them once I'd finished the work. But the months passed, and I no longer wanted to go.

I was devastated by the war that was happening out there. While one side was soon going to be celebrating victory and the other lamenting their defeat, I continued to lug along my 'mixed state' and my bitter disappointment like a ball and chain on each leg. And then I'd imagined a communal, collectivist and, above all, secular state. I couldn't bear the idea that the new state was choosing religion and individualism, because that represented everything I hated. A state religion, which came down to creating, once again, two categories of population: the Jews and the others. Had our victory over the British obscured all the ideals we'd been fighting for over the last two years? It was no use me explaining my reasons, trying to convince people—no one shared my doubts; I was the only atheist.

"Are you saying you regret what you'd done?"

Of course not. I was proud of having helped to facilitate the illegal immigration of tens of thousands of concentration camp survivors as well as of having contributed to the creation of the state of Israel, but I called M. Pol to tell him I wouldn't be going there. I explained to him that I preferred the country that had chosen secularism and issued the Declaration of the Rights of Man, even if they weren't always respected, and that I was still working underground. He took it very badly but, after all, I hadn't taken the oath to the Jewish Army; I didn't owe him anything. They all went, except me. I never saw them again, though I do know that for many years they were waiting for me to come.

Adolfo Kaminsky at age nineteen.
Self-portrait taken in the photography room, 1944.

The chemical laboratory of the 6th section and the MLN. 21, Rue Jacob, 1944.

Self-portrait of Adolfo Kaminsky in the Haganah's laboratory for forged papers, Rue d'Écosse, 1947.

Self-portrait taken in 1948 in the Forest of Fontainebleau.
Adolfo Kaminsky chose the setting as an allusion to deportation.

The dark room for developing film and for chemicals in the laboratory for forged papers in Rue des Jeûneurs. Photo taken in 1958.

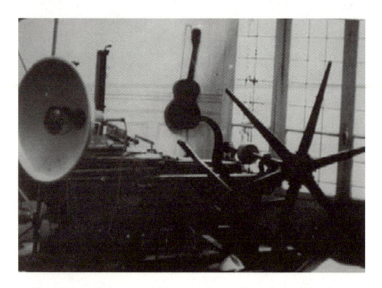

The lithographic press with its crank handle in the middle of the photographic projectors, Rue des Jeûneurs, 1958.

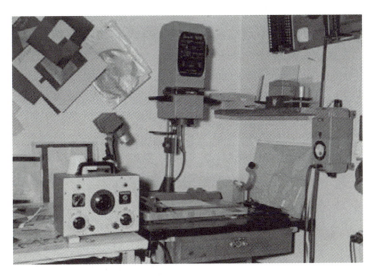

The corner for enlargements and printing,
Rue des Jeûneurs laboratory, 1960.

Adolfo Kaminsky in his Rue des Jeûneurs laboratory, 1960.

Francis Jeanson's forged papers; here, two Belgian identity cards and a Moroccan passport.

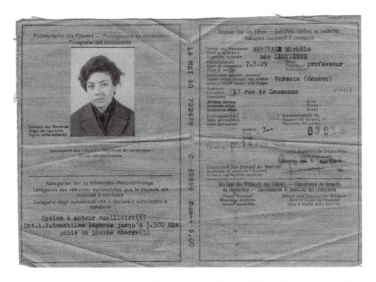

Hélène Cuenat's forged papers when she escaped from prison in 1961.
ABOVE: a Swiss driver's license. BELOW: a Swiss identity card.

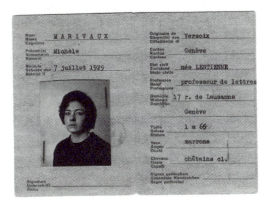

Portrait of Adolfo Kaminsky, 2009.

7

FEBRUARY 1961.

"Six women held in La Roquette Prison escaped last night: three French, two Muslim French from Algeria and one Egyptian, all active members of the support networks of the FLN.[1] They climbed over the prison walls in the middle of the night..."

A week ago it was from the nasal voice of the Paris-Inter reporter that I learned the details of the way the girls, our 'buddies', had escaped from La Roquette. I allowed myself a smile of admiration. For some time now there's been much talk of 'those French who support the Algerians', the 'bagmen' or 'the lackeys of the ragheads', depending on how sympathetic toward us they are. The gentlemen of the police in particular are taking a close interest in us. The last few months have been very trying. With the wave of arrests, the breaking up of the Jeanson network,[2] then the imprisonment of Henri Curiel,[3] those like me, who hadn't been troubled yet, spent some hard nights. Fear, euphoria,

---

1. Front de Libération Nationale, The National Liberation Front in Algeria, in the Algerian War of Independence. [MM]

2. The first French support network for the FLN that bore the name of the man who set it up, Francis Jeanson.

3. A communist Egyptian Jew who took over the organization of support for the FLN after the Jeanson network had been broken up.

days too full and nights too short, you get used to living at a hundred miles an hour, it's almost become normal.

Like every morning, I take stock of the orders in progress. My liaison agent Michèle Firk, alias 'Jeannette', is coming to collect six Belgian 'packages'—ID cards, passports, driving licenses—and four Swiss ones, of which half are completed, for the French Federation of the FLN. Yesterday I had an unexpected visit from Roland Dumas, who brought news of Francis Jeanson, still in hiding. Made very famous by his sensational trial[4] and sentenced in his absence, Francis is one of the most sought-after men in France. Roland has given me three photos of him—to be able to continue to move around he needs a French 'package'. I also have a request pending for Spanish passports for a group of Basque revolutionaries wanted by Franco's police. They'll have to wait a while longer. The most immediately urgent matter is to deal with the women who've just broken out of jail.

I put on my coat, gloves and scarf, slip the strap of my Rolleiflex round my neck. Hélène Cuenat's hideout is in the Latin Quarter, and I can get there on foot. It's windy outside, but there's also that typical winter light, a low sun sending out red and orange beams, giving the passers-by bright eyes and a shining complexion.

It's a very chic, old, freestone apartment block, with marble and mirrors in the entrance hall and a big spiral staircase covered with a richly colored carpet.

I knock at the door of the left-hand apartment on the sixth floor. "Oh, Joseph!" she cries. "Am I happy to see you!"

"Me too, very happy."

"But come in, come in, take a seat."

4. The trial of the Jeanson network was held in September 1960; six Algerians and seventeen French were accused of supporting the FLN.

While I'm making myself comfortable in one of the little arm-chairs arranged in a semicircle round the sitting room, Hélène shakes her hair and assumes the pose of a fashion model. "Well, Joseph, how do I look as a redhead? Come on, tell me what you think."

She bursts out laughing and comes to sit next to me.

"Ah well, you can't say we have a boring life," she goes on. "What a business! It wasn't all over just like that. Did you know that the cars that were supposed to pick us up when we'd gotten outside weren't there?!"

"I did hear, news travels fast. They must have had to drive off because of police patrols."

"Well... We still managed it all the same. We split up into two groups and took taxis. Just imagine, Jacqueline with only one shoe—she'd lost the other climbing the wall—and us in our dirty, threadbare, torn clothes, in the middle of the night, we must have looked like a sight!"

Hélène roars with laughter then is silent for a moment, a pensive smile on her face. She runs her fingers through her red hair before going on: "Switzerland, Belgium or anywhere else, it can't come soon enough. I'm fed up with being stuck inside."

"Exactly, that's why I'm here. You've got different outfits ready for the photos? They mustn't look as if they've all been taken on the same day."

She dumps a pile of clothes on the floor and starts to rummage around in them, like a child who's just discovered a trunk full of disguises at the back of the attic.

"I know, I know. I have to make some changes of style. I want a respectable suit, the secretary look, for crossing the border. Just look at this blouse. I'll really look uptight in that. Just what I need."

105

I move some shelves to have a section of white wall for the background to the photos and place a chair in front of it for Hélène to sit on.

"Have you already been to see the others?"

"I've only been to Jacqueline before you."

"How is she?"

"Like you, impatient. Turn your head a little to the right. Good. What shall I put as your profession on the documents?"

"Teacher."

"And for your name?"

"Michelle Marivaux, I like that."

"Chin up—perfect. That's OK, you can get changed."

The photographic session goes on. When it's time for me to leave, we find it difficult to say goodbye. I decline her invitation to stay for lunch.

"Another time, perhaps. I have too much to do today."

"Oh yes, that's right, you're always in a hurry, aren't you?"

Then, as usual, we give each other a good pair of kisses on the cheeks with no idea how many days, months or years it'll be before we see each other again; when the papers are done I won't be the one taking them to her.

When I get back to the lab there's something else I must do. I put my Rolleiflex away in the darkroom, cross the corridor and go into the machine room, so called because it houses the immense amount of equipment I use to print large-format photos for my 'official' clientele. On the right, at the very back of the room, underneath the shelves of stationary and photographic materials are my two large trunks. Or, rather, Ernest's. Out of one of them I take the huge wooden case containing the submachine gun, the machine gun and a large quantity of ammunition, leave the lab and stagger down the five floors of the apartment building. The weaponry is about to get a new owner.

A political and military terrorist organization called the OAS[5] had recently been set up. Their attacks on us were nothing new. From the very beginning the small groups that wanted Algeria to remain French had been setting off bombs to terrorize those in favor of an Algerian national state. During the Jeanson trial the lawyers defending him, Mourad Oussedik and Jacques Vergès, came out in a cold sweat every time they opened their car door. Following the publication of the Manifesto of the 121,[6] there had been bomb attacks on the homes and vehicles of numerous well- or less well-known persons. But whereas before no one claimed responsibility for the attacks, now we knew exactly who we were dealing with. The attacks were increasing in number, especially in districts where immigrants lived, and they all bore the mark of the OAS. The bars, cafés, hotels and small businesses run by Algerians had become their preferred targets.

I knew that the French Federation of the FLN had decided to dispatch a further cargo of arms, coming from Germany or Belgium, to aid the defense of the Algerians against the OAS. My liaison agent, Jeannette, was going to deliver it. She would be driving a trailer with a double floor, double ceiling and double sides, all stuffed full of weaponry.

Unfortunately, because of the time needed to camouflage all this in the interior of the vehicle, it was taking a long time to arrive.

Then I had an idea. I remembered that when I was helping

5. Organisation armée secrète—Secret Armed Organization; sometimes Organisation de l'armée secrète—Organization of the Secret Army.

6. The Manifesto of the 121 or the Declaration on the right to insubordination in the Algerian war was signed by famous French intellectuals, professors and artists. Its publication coincided with the start of the Jeanson trial and contributed to the stir it made in the media.

Brancourt in Vire, before I was deported to Drancy, I'd been asked to find a hiding place for an important batch of arms that London had parachuted in. At the foot of one of the big trees bordering the fields of an extremely kind old man, Brancourt and I had dug out a very deep hole. No one besides the two of us knew about the hiding place, and Brancourt, as I'd heard from his widow, had died in Indochina a few years after the Liberation. A few days after I'd mentioned this to Jeannette, I was visited by a young Algerian, Belkacem Rhani, a member of the French Federation of the FLN. It was a matter of getting hold of that cache from the Second World War and handing it over to the organization. After all, it wasn't such a crazy idea, there was hope that nothing had been moved. Belkacem and I traveled to Vire without delay. I found the spot at once. The field was now occupied by a large modern apartment block. We came back empty-handed.

On the other hand there were Ernest's weapons that I didn't know what to do with. A cumbersome burden I'd had to lug around with me every time I moved. How could I have gotten rid of them? Impossible just to throw them away; if I had done so, who knows who might have found and used them? How could I be sure they wouldn't be used by petty criminals or people involved in organized crime? So far, I'd preferred to keep them myself. But at that time all my friends were falling into the hands of the police, one after the other. You can imagine the risk: a simple police check would have been enough to see me behind bars as well. It was still easy to conceal my activity as a forger: it was quite reasonable for a photographer/photoengraver to have all those machines, chemicals and tools. Stamps and documents can be hidden or destroyed, zinc plates dissolved in acid. But a submachine gun, a machine gun, a revolver, cartridges, plastic and detonators? As you can see, that's more difficult.

I gave the contents of the trunks to Belkacem, except the detonators that I thought were too old, therefore dangerous. Given the weight of the weaponry, we agreed that he would make several trips to remove it, in loads of no more than fifteen to twenty kilos, so as not to attract attention when he was was carrying them on foot. The first day he left with a bag full of bullets that was so heavy it made his whole body lean over to one side. To avoid any problems on the way, I put my beautiful Roberval scales on top of the ammunition. It made it even heavier for him, but at least it explained the weight.

Belkacem came back the next day, and we repeated the scenario.

On the third day we both agreed it would be more sensible to change our strategy. Even though the street where I lived was particularly quiet, it would have seemed strange for the same man to come three days running and leave carrying the same bag, especially if the man was Algerian. At the time the police, run by Maurice Papon,[7] were very keen on hunting down people according to their racial features.

When I get down to the entrance to the block, carrying my heavy suitcase, I go along Rue des Jeûneurs, turn right into Rue du Sentier, then right again into Rue du Croissant. The rendezvous is at a baker's. No other indication. A little bell sounds when I open the door. There are three customers in front of me. I join the queue and rummage round in my pocket for some change to buy a baguette. The fat baker's wife serves the first customer, who leaves, his bread tucked under his arm. At the back a door opens

7. A French civil servant who was in charge of the police in Paris during the Nazi Occupation and into the 1960s. [MM]

a crack, then a baker appears, covered in flour, cap on his head, white clogs and apron. It's Belkacem, hardly recognizable in his disguise.

"And what will it be for you?" the baker's wife asks.

"A baguette, please."

While she's counting out the change, Belkacem gives me a sign, then goes out of the shop carrying a shopping bag full of vegetables. I thank the lady, leave and follow him. I'm three meters behind him as we turn right into Rue du Sentier, then right again. We're in Ruelle Saint-Joseph, a little alley where no one ever goes. He slows down, I hurry up. I go past him. We exchange our loads. I continue straight on toward Rue Montmartre. He turns around in order to avoid the main streets. Ernest's weapons are now going to serve the cause of Algerian independence.

8

"HOW IS IT that you came to be helping the Algerians?"

As you can well imagine, joining a network helping the Algerians didn't happen overnight. When I joined the Jeanson network I'd already been thinking about the Algerian struggle for several years. But what can you do, alone, without a network or contact, besides harping about doing something to help them while sitting around a table in the café with your buddies? To put it in a nutshell, I wanted to help but didn't know how.

But let's go back a little. In 1948, when my comrades all emigrated to Israel, I kept the Rue d'Écosse laboratory, which had all my equipment and, since I had nowhere to go, I lived there for several months, sleeping on a simple cot.

"And your family?"

The war had split it up. Each of us made his or her own life and tried to get by the best we could. My sister was getting ready to emigrate to Israel. My father and brothers were living in Paris, but we saw very little of each other.

So there I was at twenty-three, alone, without papers, with no fixed income or an 'official' past. I took on little jobs, as a photographer or dyer, but they never matched my abilities or my hopes, since I had no formal qualifications and couldn't claim any of the usual professional experience.

All my friends had left and, to overcome my loneliness, I threw myself body and soul into photography. Every night I climbed up onto the roofs of Paris to take shots of the sleeping city. That was when my artistic ambition was aroused and the laboratory of forged papers opened up again, transformed into a photographic and chemical laboratory. Gradually I started to enjoy life again.

There was a friend who often accompanied me on my nocturnal escapades. Ervin Preis was a young Hungarian, a former member of the MOI and as enthusiastic as I was. It was during a dinner arranged by his wife that Jeanine, a young, pretty student appeared in my life. All of her family, Polish Jews by origin, had perished in the extermination camps. Only Jeanine and her sister had survived, thanks to their parents' ingenious idea of finding them positions as maids in German households.

A few months after we met, Jeanine and I were married. Our daughter Marthe was born in 1950, her little brother Serge one year later. However, it only took two years for our marriage to fail miserably. Too many misunderstandings put an end to our love. I went back to the cot in Rue d'Écosse, surrounded by my chemicals and machines.

I can only describe the years that followed as unsettled. I often changed my address, my job and my partner as well. In reality, my reintegration into 'normal' life proved difficult. My childhood shortened by the war, the years underground, the people I hadn't been able to save and Drancy had marked me indelibly. I couldn't accept that all that was over for me, and my nightmares were haunted by too many faces.

Professionally I had better and worse times—they varied.

Eventually I took a permanent job with a firm that did photographic work, for whom I specialized in giant-format photos for cinema sets. Completely independent and working closely with the directors and designers, I would go off to take the shots with a wide-angle 18 x 24 camera I lugged around and, after having developed and printed them out, I would go and stick them up in the cinema studios. I was lucky enough to take photos for the sets of Alexandre Trauner,[1] the celebrated designer for the films of Marcel Carné.

As always, I wasn't interested in routine work. What I enjoyed was solving technical problems, learning new processes, doing research.

When I set up on my own, one of my very first clients was the architect and Marxist town planner Anatole Knopp. He would order large-format pictures for information stands, shop windows, the façades of the pavilions at the *fête de l'Huma*,[2] or historical exhibitions on subjects that interested me such as the Commune, the life of Romain Rolland[3] or the coal mines of northern France.

Then I specialized in the reproduction of works of art. Meticulous, painstaking, technical work. All the things I liked. The majority of my clientele were my painter friends, South American for the most part, kinetic artists very active in the area of abstract geometric painting and Op Art. Unfortunately Oswaldo Vigas, Yaacov Agam, Jesús Soto, Carmelo Arden-Quin or Antonio Asis were not artists who are recognized today. Very often—not to say almost all the time—I had to ignore unpaid bills.

1. Trauner was the preferred set designer for most American film directors working in Europe, including Billy Wilder, Fred Zinnemann, and John Huston. Trauner was also Jewish and managed to do some work with Marcel Carné during the occupation of France by the Nazis. [MM]

2. An annual fundraising event organized by *L'Humanité*, a daily newspaper that formerly had close links with the Communist Party but is now independent. [MM]

3. A French author (1866-1944) deeply involved in the Dreyfus affair—which revealed anti-Semitism in the French army—and in the search for world peace. [MM]

In the summers of 1953 and 1954 I went twice to Algeria with Colette, my partner at the time and a photographer like me, whose father, a Greek businessman, had been living in Algeria for a long time. It was one of the more, let's say, prosperous periods in my life. Colette and I were living in a little disused factory that would nowadays be called a loft and that we also used as a photographic studio. We made photos for interior decoration, shop windows, and advertising for chain stores.

Thanks to this steady clientele, we had regular commissions and even time to go on summer vacations. She used to go and visit her father as often as possible, and in those two years I accompanied her. Over there I saw the serious problems caused by colonization. I became acutely aware of the distinction between the two categories of population, the French on the one hand and the 'French Muslims of Algeria'—as people said at the time when they were being polite, although the word 'Arabs' came more automatically to their lips—on the other. I saw the racism, the discrimination, the public humiliation. I saw the Algerians being addressed by the familiar 'tu' while the French were called 'Monsieur'. Faced with scenes that made me feel very uncomfortable, I was often ashamed of my status as a white person. I was ashamed for France.

It would be an untruth to generalize and say that everyone was racist. I did of course also meet some marvelous people who even fought for civil rights equality between the French and the 'natives'. In fact it was from them that I learned that they didn't have the same rights and that French law made them into a sub-category: the French had the right to vote but not the French Muslims. But when I was at school hadn't I learned that Algeria was France? So what did that say about the 'equality' between citizens?

I regarded this magnificent country with its infinitely rich culture as a pressure cooker ready to explode. The condescending attitude of the majority of the French in Algeria toward the Algerians, the paternalistic proprietorial relationship to quasi-slaves, could only fan the flames of this well-stoked fire. Colette and I took photos of Algiers and the very beautiful faces of children looking at us from behind bars. These photographs showed all the beauty and gravity of Algeria.

The first day of the insurrection, November 1, 1954 went more or less unnoticed in France. There was talk of terrorists, of attacks. As for me, I wasn't fooled, as I had been during the uprising of May 8, 1945, during the first demonstration for the independence of Algeria that coincided with the capitulation of Germany. At the time, the press had made no mention of the slaughter of several hundred civilians. The event had been presented as an outpouring of hatred by extremist, anti-Semitic and anti-French Muslims, who were demonstrating their support for defeated Nazi Germany. I'd believed it.

As you will know, for years no one talked of the 'war' in Algeria. It was the departure of the first servicemen who'd been called up again[4] and the propaganda about the 'pacification' of Algeria that opened my eyes and really disturbed me. As far as I remember, for me the war began then, even though the lying official discourse was doing its best to conceal the fact: if there was no war why send all those young people there? I felt solidarity with the recalled soldiers who were demonstrating because I was already firmly convinced that France was sending her children to the slaughterhouse. And very angry with the representatives of the

4. Cohorts of young people who had completed their military service less than three years previously were recalled in their thousands in order to 'pacify' Algeria. When they got there it was war they were faced with.

left: apart from the Trotskyists of the PCI[5] and the left-wing Christians, no one declared openly for Algerian independence. The Communist Party? Silence. The French section of the Workers' International? Forget it.

It was during this time that I met a young black American woman, Sarah Elizabeth Penn from New York, at an end-of-shooting party organized by the filmmaker Jean Rouch. We stayed together the whole evening. She gabbled in her delightful 'franglais', drank and danced, laughed at her own clumsiness and at mine. By the end of the evening I was madly in love. Quite simply love at first sight. At that time my schedule wasn't particularly full, and it so happened that I'd just been hired by a photographic firm specializing in tourist posters and picture postcards, for which I was getting ready to go off on an assignment, a seven-month trip along the coasts of Europe.

"Do you want to come with me?" I asked her when we'd hardly known each other for a few weeks.

With a flutter of eyelashes, she agreed, and we set off in a Renault 4CV. We camped, erecting our tent wherever we found a little patch of paradise. I took my photos very early in the morning and spent the rest of the day showing Sarah Elizabeth the landscapes and towns we were passing through; she marveled at everything. The lack of comfort didn't matter, for the very first time my life was a perfect idyll with not a cloud on the horizon. We understood each other. I taught her how to take photos, she painted some very beautiful portraits and made jewels of African inspiration. True, we weren't rich at all but we were artists, free and happy! This Bohemian life suited both of us. We worked in silence, side by side; at the end of the day and late into the night we were

5. Parti communiste internationaliste (International Communist Party), a Trotskyist organization and French section of the Fourth International. [MM]

making plans for the future. We could already see ourselves enjoying artistic success, in France, perhaps in the United States. We even went so far as to imagine what our future children would look like, and all this made me forget my Parisian concerns, the worries of everyday life. Politics and everything that was at stake—peace and war—blotted out. After two years with Sarah Elizabeth, of which half the time was spent going up and down the coasts, the question of moving to the States became more and more urgent. I started talking about it to my employer who, after having tried everything to keep me in Paris, made me an offer I'd hardly dared hope for: a trial period with his firm in the United States followed by a position over there.

Sarah Elizabeth went first, in order to see her family again. We'd agreed I'd follow four months later, at the beginning of 1958, to give me time to get myself sorted out, to sell everything I owned or give it to friends to look after. I put the news around: I was going to America...

Four months is a long time. First of all there were the congratulations and the 'we'll come and see you, that's a promise', then life went on and political discussions came to the fore again. For time was passing, and the confrontations in Algeria were stepping up. I was more and more concerned but still hadn't found a way of becoming more involved.

The conflict set off a series of consequences in France. Paris was beginning to feel the effect of the Algerian drama: the hunt for racial characteristics, constant police checks. Personally I didn't know any Algerians, but my South American friends told me they were often taken in for questioning because of their Mediterranean appearance. To me, it was absolutely intolerable that the French authorities should be hunting for people with a swarthy complexion, just as the Nazis had been on the lookout for the Jewish nose a few years previously.

Toward the end of 1957 the first reports on the use of torture by the French army and police in Algeria appeared. We knew about it already, but this time it was no longer a matter of isolated actions. Several high-ranking officers had refused to be party to it and had even asked to be relieved of their duties. There were some of us, former members of the Resistance, who saw the specter of the Gestapo reappearing. The victims were different but the methods the same. The 'suicide' of the lawyer Ali Boumendjel[6] and the disappearance of Maurice Audin[7] confirmed the fact that in Algeria people were being tortured and killed with impunity. On top of that there was the censorship. Anyone who wrote even a brief article on the question or on the independence of Algeria was immediately arrested, their home searched, their writings confiscated and destroyed. I was very worried about young people, the deserters who were risking being sent to prison for life by following their conscience. But I was even more worried for those who didn't have the courage to choose insubordination. What was going to become of them?

Torturers? Heroes who'd given their lives for their country? In either case France was sacrificing her children for nothing, for Algeria had long been lost.

At that time I was a regular in the cafés of Montparnasse and Boulevard Saint-Germain. I went to listen to South American music in *L'Escale*, to have a coffee in the *Flore*, the *Sélect*, *La*

---

6. An Algerian lawyer tortured and killed by the French army in Algeria in March 1957.

7. A French mathematician teaching at the University of Algiers; he was a member of the Communist Party and a militant anti-colonialist who disappeared in circumstances that have never been cleared up after having been arrested at his home by the French authorities.

Rhumerie martiniquaise and, above all, in the *Old Navy*, a meeting place where many filmmakers, journalists and other intellectuals would drop in. I would be there every evening from eight o'clock onward. I had my table there, received mail and telephone calls, arranged meetings, met my friends, mostly painters and film people, the journalist Georges Arnaud, the writer Arthur Adamov, a fair number of wannabes full of ambition and lots of pretty girls. Concerned about what was going on in Algeria, we talked passionately about what had to be done, but in concrete terms we didn't do very much.

In the autumn of 1957 I celebrated my thirty-second birthday. Marcelline Loridan—a friend I met there to whom I told my life-story after she'd told me hers; a survivor of Birkenau concentration camp, she had come back at seventeen, a tattoo forever engraved on her skin, full of the energy of desperation—introduced me to Annette Roger. A doctor from Marseilles, Annette was a pretty blonde, slim and elegant, with tremendous drive. We very quickly hit it off, and she was happy to accept my suggestion that she come over the next day to pose for a series of portraits I was working on.

It was a rather strange photographic session. There was no question about the quality of the model; she was absolutely perfect. The truth is that we hardly worked at all. Annette was the sort of person who is very, very curious. She wanted to discuss things. I quickly realized that Marcelline must have told her about the stuff I'd done with forged documents during the Occupation, for she immediately brought it up. Since she wanted to know the details, I told her everything in a long monologue. The Second World War. The army secret service. The Haganah and the Stern group. When I'd finished there were a few seconds of silence between us. Then she took a deep breath.

"And now? Could you still make forged papers?" she asked, looking me straight in the eye.

"If it's justified by the cause."

With the faintest of smiles, she said, "I think you're the man we need. How do you feel about meeting Francis Jeanson?"

Francis Jeanson, called 'the Professor', I already knew by name. Anyone in the left-wing intellectual circles around me who was interested in the Algerian question had read or heard about the book he'd written together with his wife: *L'Algérie hors la loi* (Algeria outside the law). And now and then I used to read Jean-Paul Sartre's philosophical journal *Les Temps modernes* (Modern Times), and I knew that he had been its editor. I'd also heard that he'd fallen out with Camus for having written a not very favorable review of his novel *The Stranger*. While personally I saw nothing wrong with the literary quality of Camus' book, I'd also argued with him some years previously in the course of a heated conversation about Algeria in which I'd criticized him for being so lukewarm about it. I was, therefore, quite keen to put a face to the name. The encounter took place in Marcelline's apartment in the Latin Quarter. When I entered the room where he was waiting for me, I was surprised to find I recognized him. A few years previously I'd been in the apartment of Romain Rolland's widow, where I was making reproductions of some archive photographs for a book on her husband's life, when she was visited by a rather timid journalist who wanted to interview her. It was Francis Jeanson. By now there was nothing timid about Francis. On the contrary he displayed striking determination and energy.

Francis was an astonishing character. An intellectual, an

existentialist philosopher, his doctrine was based on the idea that thought should not be dissociated from action or, if you prefer, that anti-colonialism should not be restricted to standing on the sidelines keeping the score. He took an interest in the cause of the Algerians at two points in his life. First of all under the Occupation. Having enlisted in the Free French Army of Africa during the Second World War, he found that the majority of French Algerians were Vichyists, even collaborationists. Then he went back there with his wife in 1948. He wanted to live closer to the Muslims, to share in their daily life. That was the time when he met some militant nationalists. He emphasizes that his decision to commit himself totally to them was taken as a Frenchman, in order to keep alive the possibility of Franco-Algerian friendship, to give a wake-up call to the French left wing and equally because, like me, he was convinced from the very beginning that the people of Algeria would achieve independence, with the help of France or against her. His idea was to help the Algerians win the war as quickly as possible, so as to avoid the pointless loss of human lives on both sides. He asked me if I was willing to join the network.

"Of course," I replied.

"Yes, but to *really* join us," he said.

"What do you mean, really?"

"Full time. Do the printing. Be able to respond to urgent requests. Lots of documents, different nationalities. And the famous Swiss passport, impossible to forge."

Francis then set off on an interminable list of the forged documents they would need. I'd never imagined their requirements would be so important. Francis' voice was like a muffled hubbub in the background, while my thoughts were with Sarah

Elizabeth, who was waiting for me in the United States...

One week later I had a rendezvous with Jeanson's right-hand man in *La Rhumerie martiniquaise*.

"Daniel," he said by way of introduction, as he stood up to shake my hand before inviting me to take a seat.

Very middle class. Tall and strong, elegant in a suit and dark tie, suntanned, as if he'd just come back from vacation, distinguished looking, a fine-leather briefcase on his knees. He finished off his whisky before calling the waiter. A second whisky for him. For me a white coffee.

We were immediately on friendly terms, calling each other '*tu*' right from the start, and we introduced ourselves briefly. 'Daniel'—Jacques Vignes by his real name—came from Bordeaux and was a childhood friend of Francis Jeanson. He was a quiet man with a wife and family, a keen sailor, a specialist in yacht racing and a sports journalist when the fancy took him, and before joining the network he'd managed, with no great enthusiasm, a small family business selling bathroom furniture. He told me he hadn't hesitated for one second when Francis Jeanson had asked him to be his right-hand man and to take charge of all the organization of the network and the coordination of the escape routes. And for that his main problem was crossing borders. Until then, in order to get money, Algerian leaders, wanted people or deserters out of the country, Daniel had always used the Spanish border. At that time, when the war was intensifying, the number of deserters increasing, fund-raising becoming more widespread and systematic, it was a matter of some urgency to increase the access routes using all the possibilities offered by neighboring countries: Spain, Italy, Switzerland, Germany and Belgium. The money that was essential to support the insurrection was collected, sorted and counted in

France, but could only be deposited in Switzerland. So from that point on Daniel would be my contact and would soon be needing Spanish, Italian, Swiss, German, Belgian and French papers for wanted people and the network's agents whose job it was to cross borders.

When I left, he gave me an envelope containing his first order, insisted on paying for our drinks and arranged for us to meet again in two days' time.

As I made my way home, I felt a bit perplexed. What did I feel about this first meeting? We'd talked for a little over an hour. Like Jeanson, like myself and all those who'd joined the network, he had taken on the commitment as a Frenchman, for the sake of the Franco-Algerian friendship that had to be established because the French values of 'liberty-equality-fraternity' ought to inform the campaign, because it was inevitable that Algeria would eventually be independent, and we had to help them win the battle as quickly as possible if we wanted to stop the waste, stop sending our boys over there to die, and so that we didn't entirely lose the trust of our Algerian brothers. His convictions were sincere and his reading of events pertinent, and yet there was something that bothered me. I found it impossible to assess this first contact as positive. When I'd left, he was on his third whisky. I had the impression his voice was no longer clear, that he was stumbling over his words, stammering... I don't know, what he said was still coherent, but three whiskies in the morning? Could the organization of a network rest on his shoulders? I was skeptical. To be honest I even thought that frankly it wasn't something that could be taken seriously. Oh, if I'd only known back then.

Remember this lesson: don't always trust your first impressions. I'd just met one of the most efficient behind-the-scenes men

I've known in my whole career.

In the hall of the apartment block I glance at my mail. No bills, just a letter. I could recognize that handwriting anywhere. Sarah Elizabeth's handwriting is round and two to three times larger than anyone else's. Immediately my heart sinks. I go up the stairs and put both the envelopes on the table. Daniel's: A4, heavy brown paper. Sarah Elizabeth's: cancelled U.S. stamp, white, long and slim, linen-wove, bound with Scotchtape—she'd obviously made it herself.

On the window ledge Bishken is cheeping, thinking I've forgotten him. I take a little piece of stale bread out of my pocket and crumble it up for him while he whistles his thanks. Like every day, he'll eat it all, fly off and come back the next. How she loved that bird...

It's the fourth letter I've had since she left. I just can't get around to replying. In her last letter—envelope hand-painted, flesh-colored embossed cardboard, fountain pen on tracing paper inside, ten pages long because she decorates each page with illustrations and annotations—she asked, "Why don't you write anymore? I'd like to know who's replacing me while I'm waiting. Have you started selling your things? I tell my friends about you. Don't forget to buy the Scotch for my father on the boat. Everyone's looking forward to seeing you. Write back."

What's she going to say to me in this one? I'm not sure I want to know.

These last few days I've had to make one of the hardest choices possible: her or them? Love or the cause? We'd arranged everything perfectly: she would leave first to see her family while I would stay on a few months to tie up my affairs, sell everything I had and train the new photographer who was going to replace me. There was even work waiting for me over there that my boss was keeping for me in a subsidiary company. How could I tell her I wouldn't be coming? I'd drafted hundreds of letters to explain my silence, but every time I just didn't seem to have the strength to stick the stamp on. There were so many things to say, to explain, to reveal, and my replies were so poor, so incomplete, I'd have to go back to the beginning and start all over again. How could she, who'd never known anything about my political activities, understand my commitment?

Bishken's gone without my noticing and without leaving a crumb. In the end I don't open Sarah Elizabeth's letter but drop it in a drawer to join all her other letters and all the replies I've drafted.

Instead I open Daniel's. It contains a Belgian identity card and driver's license that I'm to tamper with, not forge; that is, I just have to replace the photos and change the dates of birth and the professions. Using documents belonging to someone else, stolen, lent or 'lost' with their agreement, is like the work I did when I first joined the Resistance. Just tinkering. I have to analyze the ink, delete it and write in the new data over it. The photo's just stapled on, but it has a relief stamp across the corner, half on the boards. The revenue stamp is half underneath the photo, and it's been stamped as well, this time with ink, not in relief but flat.

It so happens that I still have all my chemicals, my coloring agents. I even have photoengraving plates and acid. Pure products don't deteriorate.

I start by making a metal alloy of my own invention that has a very low melting point. Once it has liquefied, since it isn't hot, I can just deposit the alloy on the documents—on the relief stamp, to be exact—then let it harden. For the flat stamp I use an ink that contains a little glycerin, since that makes it stay wet, and I can copy with precision the missing part of the stamp on non-absorbent tracing paper. Then I place the tracing paper on paper with a coating of gelatin, which I will use as the final stamp. Now I can replace the photo with Daniel's.

All that is left is to change the date of birth and profession. I analyze the ink. It uses a black aniline coloring agent, a very common ink that you have to oxidize to remove, then neutralize it with ammoniac vapor. I make a solution of permanganate of potash and bisulfite of soda. The owner of the documents is an electrician, and I assume Daniel has no knowledge in that area. I have to find something else. On reflection I choose the profession of sales rep, which suits him well. With ink of the same composition I enter the new details meticulously, imitating precisely the handwriting of the clerk in the mayor's office who filled out the papers, and that's that. My first forged documents for the Jeanson network, the French support network for the FLN, are ready.

It's been ages since I've made any forged papers. The last time was in 1950, seven years ago. The Stern group, declared illegal in Israel, had been hunted down and condemned for terrorism. As a one-off I'd supplied forged documents for my friends who were sought by the authorities and who wanted to come back to France.

Alone at home, I examine and reexamine the ID card and the driver's license. I'm pretty satisfied. I haven't lost my touch— the result is absolutely perfect.

9

IT WAS THE FIRST TIME Francis Jeanson and Daniel had been shown around the Rue des Jeûneurs laboratory. Usually, when one of them came to leave a request I attended to them quickly in the waiting room, took the envelope and accompanied them to the door. I wasn't a chatty type. But that day they wanted to 'see'.

Just imagine: a laboratory of more than a hundred and fifty square meters. First of all you have to go down a long corridor leading onto a waiting room on the left, then three doors on the right and one at the end. I'd turned the first room on the right into a darkroom for developing the film: a line of eight tanks against one wall, the same number of clocks with electric bells, set according to the processing time, and the same number of thermometers standing in the tanks. The next door leads into a kitchen that had been made into the room for the 'machines', containing the bulky appliances for glazing and washing the photos. At the end, the large main laboratory. Windows blocked up and covered in black, the lighting red and green. My four, big, color and black-and-white enlargers are set up on tables with drawers for the paper, films and work in progress. The drying cupboard, light boxes, broad working surfaces, a guillotine, a spectrometer, magnifying glasses, a microscope, infrared and ultraviolet lamps. Against the back wall, four aligned sinks contain basins for damping and bathing, with all the chemicals set out above them. Above everything, washing lines for drying films, photos, and documents stretch all the way down the room.

At the back there's another door leading to the large print room. In pride of place, under a large plate-glass window right in the middle of the room, is my big litho press, a genuine museum piece that I'd kept in separate pieces for years. On a table against one of the walls is the lithographic stone, on which the inks are spread and, along the whole wall all the inking rollers in a rack. More work surfaces, zinc plates and instruments for cutting them and mounting them on the stone, guillotines, a home-made laminator to reduce the thickness of the paper, shelves on the walls for the inks and the colors.

Beyond that is a door leading to a big attic. On the right, our stocks. On the left, the vast photographic studio that also serves as a bedroom and sitting room.

By another door you can continue around. It takes you to the dining room, then back to the waiting room and the entrance corridor. My lair. My laboratory.

Life sometimes springs some strange surprises on us. You remember Goumard, the photoengraver who was in the Resistance but hated foreigners? Well, it was partly thanks to him that I obtained those premises. When I joined the Jeanson network my first priority was to set up a proper laboratory. At home, in my tiny two-room apartment turned into a studio after I'd given over the bedroom to stock all my material, it was impossible to do good work.

So I went out looking for a place where I could. And, as usual,

I hadn't a penny. Francis had suggested paying me a salary because he suspected he'd be needing me full time and also so that I could meet any technical expenses, but I refused, and that for two reasons. Firstly because it was difficult to determine in advance the cost of running a laboratory, given that I didn't yet know how frequent the requests would be, but also, and above all, because in accepting payment I would have the feeling I'd become a mercenary. More than anything else, I was determined to preserve my independence. If the network should move in a direction I didn't approve of, for example by organizing terrorist attacks on civilians, I would be free to leave.

But freedom has its price. I had to give up my job and go back to working for myself, create a photography firm to reconcile my two activities, legal and illegal.

Quite by chance, I had business in the district around the Stock Exchange and happened to see a little notice taped to a wall announcing a lease being put up for auction. When I went to see the premises, they were a complete ruin. The former tenant, a press agency, had gone bankrupt. It was horribly dirty, the wall eaten away by splashes of fixative; everything was rotten. No one wanted it. But I did. I fell for it right away. For a start, the rent was ridiculously low, and it was a joint tenancy. The premises consisted of half of the top floor of the building, and I immediately saw that the other half was unoccupied and that there were two different staircases to get up there. Very practical to avoid meeting people or, should it be necessary, making a discreet exit.

I went to see Monsieur Petit, the lawyer, a stiff, authoritarian person, well past sixty. I explained that I wanted the premises and that I hoped he would reserve it for me, giving me time to set up my firm so I could sign the lease.

"How much time?" he asked.

"I don't know. As I'm a foreigner the first thing I have to do is to find a managing director."

When he heard the word 'foreigner', M. Petit frowned as if I'd just said something obscene.

"Where do you come from?"

"Argentina."

"And what kind of firm are you going to set up?"

"Technical and color photography. Photoengraving as well."

He was suddenly overcome by a memory that didn't seem too unpleasant. "I know a bit about photoengraving," he said. "I had a friend, now unfortunately deceased, who was a photoengraver. But he was one of the best. He taught at École Estienne."

"What was his name?"

"Henri Goumard."

"I knew him as well. He taught me."

From then on M. Petit took a liking to me. Since I'd been a pupil of his dear departed friend, he decided to take matters in hand himself and to help me. He gave me the keys right away so that I could start renovating the place. As far as the firm was concerned, he suggested that his son, a gentleman of around forty who worked with him while reading *Minute*,[1] should officially be the managing director, at least on paper. The FLN forger having as managing director a man who sympathized with the extreme right—I couldn't have dreamed of better cover.

Francis and Daniel had been astounded when they went through the laboratory and asked thousands of questions. It's true that there was something impressive about it. I'd just

1. An extremely right-wing weekly magazine. [MM]

explained to them how, using a stereotype block, you can do photolithography and shown them how to get a reaction from the ink after mixing in some color. But what fascinated them most of all was my archive box containing all the ID cards and stamps going back to the Second World War and the collective visas for the Haganah.

"You claim that there's nothing that's impossible to forge, don't you?" Francis asked, examining a visa for Brazil with a magnifying glass.

"That's right. Anything that's been conceived and made by one man can naturally be reproduced by another."

"We have an urgent request for two Swiss passports for the day after tomorrow."

The famous Swiss passports. Since I'd been making forged documents again, I hadn't come across any major difficulties besides the time limits stipulated, which had initially been difficult to stick to, though having to start right from the beginning again had been a long and tedious task. French identity cards, driver's licenses, passports were not at all like what they'd been up to 1950, which meant that I had no valid model, plates or stamps. But the Swiss passport was a veritable technical challenge, and I wasn't sure I could meet it. The texture of the cover, ultra-light boards that were both rigid and very supple with relief watermarks, was unlike that of any other passport in the world. No one had ever been able to reproduce it, and I had just two days to find a solution!

Without wasting a minute, I shut myself away in the lab and, as usual, tried everything, with different combinations of paper, cellulose, glue. Unfortunately the first tests were very disappointing. I could get either the suppleness or the rigidity, but never both at the same time. I had to keep going back to the beginning again, persevere, try new proportions...

One day and one night had gone, and I still didn't have the least idea how to do it. I walked up and down the laboratory, fighting against sleep. It wasn't the time for weakness. But my weariness was suddenly followed by a violent headache, a sensation like a needle stabbing me just behind the eyes, a sharp pain that took my breath away. Impossible to fight against it. I immediately stretched out on the wooden bench, waiting for it to pass. And in closing my eyes, I let go and allowed myself to be literally carried away by sleep. Believe it or not, my mind went on working while I was asleep. In my dream I continued my experiments with other types of paper, adding cellulose in tiny quantities, and, perhaps because of the headache and the fact that I hadn't had time to take an aspirin, by some devious piece of serendipity I remembered that gauze dressings contained a lot of pure cellulose. I dreamed that I cut up pieces and incorporated them in some pulp I'd made myself from different types of paper chosen for their resemblance to the model before dissolving them in a basic solution. Once the paper had dried I examined the result. Unbelievable!

I immediately woke with a start. I was aching all over from having slept on the wood, but my headache was gone. How long had I been dozing? It was already dark outside. All I had left was the night and the morning. I dashed into the bathroom, opened the big medicine cupboard and rummaged around inside. Gauze dressings... Was it possible? If it was, there was perhaps still hope, however minimal, that the passports would be ready in time.

I proceeded in exactly the same way as in my dream, chopped up the gauze into small pieces and incorporated it into the pulp after having dissolved it. After letting it emulsify for half an hour or so, I obtained a pulp that matched up to my expectations and put the sheets in the drying cupboard. The drying process was interminable, and I spent the hours pacing up and down. As dawn was breaking I still had to laminate the layers to get a regular thickness that was the same as in the model, and finally I could compare them.

My sheets had exactly the same texture to the eye, the consistency was identical in all respects to the touch and even under the microscope it was impossible to pick out the least fault, the least trace that it had been forged. All that was left now was to color, print, and cut them, then insert the pages of the passport. And tomorrow, I thought with a smile, I'll go to the pharmacy to buy lots and lots of gauze...

10

IN THE MILD ATMOSPHERE and the evening light falling through the large skylight, I turn the heavy crank handle of the press while Marie-Aline collects the printed sheets as they come out. Suddenly the silence is broken by the baby's cries.

"She's woken up, we'll take a break," Marie-Aline sighs as she goes to get her daughter.

Now I'm making lots of Swiss passports. Their reputation as impossible to forge ensures that many risky operations go well. It was many years later that I learned that in reality Francis and Daniel had lied when they came to ask for the first Swiss passports: they didn't need any at all. They were both intrigued by the fact that at every request, even the most complicated ones, even with the shortest deadline, I would take the model without a word and produce the goods on time. They wanted to set me an impossible task to hear me say, if only once, "I can't do it." Sure that I would fail, they were going to tell me the truth then. When I took them the two passports, they felt stupid and accepted them without daring to say anything. And quite right too. I only learned the truth of the story several decades later. A stupid joke, yes, but one that ultimately saved me a lot of time because the

Swiss passport was precious, and the organization very soon really needed them.

Marie-Aline suddenly reappears, a feeding bottle in one hand, a diaper in the other and little Nathalie, still crying, clutching her around the neck.

"I'm going to have to feed her. And give her her bath, too, before the babysitter arrives." Marie-Aline burst into my life like a flower in spring. One day we didn't know each other at all; the next we were living together as if it had always been like that. One evening in the *Old Navy* a woman friend had said to me, "Tell me, Adolphe, you wouldn't have some work for a pal of mine who needs a bit of cash?" I'd just signed the lease for the lab in Rue des Jeûneurs, and it was black with grime. All I could suggest was a few francs for giving me a hand with the housework. The next day a slip of a woman of around twenty-five appeared at the door pushing her blond locks, which were falling over her big blue eyes, behind her ears.

"I'm called Marie-Aline, I've come to do the housework."

She was bubbly, amusing and never at a loss for words. She came to work and never left. A few days later I learned that she was a single mother and needed the money to pay the nurse who was looking after her daughter until she could take her back. I made a cot that I put beside our bed in the photographic studio, and we went to fetch Nathalie. What with setting up my photography firm and the clandestine printing press, that made quite a lot of things to deal with at the same time. Although she was very committed politically and very strongly supported the Algerian struggle, Marie-Aline was still unaware of my double activity. How could I conceal it when we lived, slept, ate and worked in the same place? I had to tell her. Initially she was scared stiff, imagining the police turning up at any time of the day or night to arrest us. Then she overcame her fears and decided to help me, between feeding times.

The bell rings. I pick up the last sheet from the press and carefully put it away in the drawer. I lock the doors of the print room, the store, the main lab and the room with the machines, before opening the door for the baby-sitter. Aurélie, a young Eurasian girl of fifteen or sixteen with a gentle, sad look comes into the corridor and timidly introduces herself. It's a friend who suggested her because since the baby arrived we haven't been going out very much. While Marie-Aline is telling her where everything is and I'm having one last check that there's nothing compromising in sight, the telephone rings. "Adolphe, there's something I have to talk to you about. Are you free tomorrow?" It's Henri, a photographer friend, on the line.

"Yes."

"See you at the *Saint-Claude* at five."

As soon as we arrive at the *Old Navy*, the owner calls out to me, "Mail for you."

The envelope has the American flag painted over it, and it's addressed to 'M. le Patron de l'*Old Navy*, Boulevard Saint-Germain, France'. On an A3 sheet, folded over eight times, Sarah Elizabeth has written just one sentence: "Tell Adolphe America's waiting for him." I'd finally got around to telling her I wouldn't be coming, suggesting she come back to live in Paris. But she hadn't understood. How could she, since I couldn't reveal to her the torments that kept me in France? In her reply she'd demanded explanations and, unable to give her any, with a bitter feeling I'd broken off communication.

136

"Hey, just look at you!" Marie-Aline exclaimed, all smiles and tugging at my sleeve. "Claude wants to see you, come on, come on."

Claude Ravard, sitting at a table right at the back of the café, waves me over. I weave my way through the crowd of customers, shaking a few hands and pecking a few cheeks as I go. Claude has an odd expression on his face; he looks upset.

"You don't seem like yourself today."

"I have a problem to sort out by tomorrow, perhaps you can help me," he said, swirling the ice cubes around in his glass.

"Go ahead and tell me."

"I've been asked to take in a wanted Algerian. A big shot. The problem is, I've already got one in my pad. I've got until tomorrow to find a new hideout."

I was the one who'd introduced Claude to the network. Lodgings were one of our priorities because wanted Algerians were systematically rounded up if they stayed in a hotel. Nor could they eat in restaurants or take the risk of going around on foot. Jacques Charby, an actor who was very committed to the cause, had set up a very efficient network of lodgings by prospecting among his friends, people from the theater. The one problem was that different Algerians couldn't keep on going to the same apartment one after the other, so we were constantly looking for new places for them to stay. One day Francis and Daniel asked me about lodgings that could be arranged outside Jacques Charby's list, and I'd immediately thought of Claude. A union official with the Air France branch of the CGT[1] he was more than willing, on condition he was left out of the network. As a member of the Communist Party he had to keep his activity

1. The Confédération générale du travail (General Confederation of Labor) is a French trade union. [MM]

secret if he didn't want to risk being excluded from the party, as all those who had publicly stood up for Algerian independence had been.

"It appears that it's not just anybody," Claude went on, emptying his glass. "A very senior official, he needs somewhere that's really secure, somewhere no one will think of going to look for him."

"I may have an idea. If you like, I'll deal with it."

When we get back, everything's quiet in the house. Marie-Aline and I go in, treading softly. The light from the few street lamps shines through the windows. Nathalie's sound asleep in her cot. Aurélie the babysitter is also dozing, on the wooden bench. With an amused glance at me, Marie-Aline shrugs her shoulders, then takes a blanket from the cupboard and tucks it around the girl.

The next day I go out early in the morning. I have a full day ahead. I have to solve Claude's lodging problem, then, at five as arranged, I'll go to the *Saint-Claude* to see Henri, my photographer friend who'd called me the previous day. But before all of that I have another matter to sort out. More money problems I have to deal with. I've just paid the rent for the laboratory. I have absolutely nothing left, and I've run out of inks, chemicals and paper.

At the state pawnbroker's the assistant welcomes me. Not many of my friends are aware of this, but I'm well known here, at the 'hockshop'. For a Rolleiflex they offer me hardly one tenth of its value. I leave one there, plus a 24 x 36 Exakta that I'll come back to reclaim as soon as I can pay the interest. For a while I'd managed to coordinate my double activity, but it didn't last. At first I divided my time fifty-fifty; the orders for photographs, invoiced, allowed me to do those for the FLN documents free of charge.

Now I'm working almost a hundred percent for the FLN, my coffers are empty, and I'm running up debts.

Because of this detour I had to make, it's already midday when I arrive at an old friend's. Philippe gives me a warm welcome in his immense, very middle-class apartment in the 16th arrondissement.[2] When Claude asked me to find a secure place where no one would think of looking for an Algerian, it was Philippe who immediately occurred to me. To have a senior official of the FLN who's on the run lodging with a Jew who's in favor of Algeria remaining French is a bit daring, don't you think? But it's impossible to imagine a better hideout. A former member of the Resistance and of the MJS, after the war Philippe went to live in Algeria with a branch of his family, Jews who had lived in the country for several generations. The events there had finally impelled him to return to Paris; since then, he had been proclaiming his support for French Algeria loud and clear. No, really, no one would think of looking for the FLN in his apartment.

As we haven't seen each other for several years, we talk and talk, go on and on about stories from the past before coming back to the present and the problem that's brought me there.

No sooner have I mentioned the word FLN than Philippe gets up out of his chair, red with fury, shouting at me, "That's a lousy thing to ask of me because you know very well that I can't refuse."

"Yes, you can refuse. Say yes or no, and if it's no, we'll say no more about it," I retort, once his angry shouts have died down.

"After everything you've done for me? You saved my life. You saved my father, my mother and my sister. I can't say no!"

"Say yes, then."

"I warn you, Adolphe, once but not twice."

I still feel a bit worked up about this when, one hour later I push open the door of the *Saint-Claude* and plunge into the quiet

2. A district of Paris socially similar to New York's Upper East Side. [MM]

139

hubbub of the café. Henri's there already, leaning on the bar.

"Let's go in the back room, it'll be quieter there," he suggests, pointing to a table in a corner.

We're the only ones in the back room. Leaning on the table, Henri gets close to me and speaks in a very low voice: "I've been contacted by the Algerians."

"Oh, yes?" I say without batting an eyelid. There's no way Henri can know I'm helping the FLN. Apart from Marie-Aline and a few others, no one's aware of that.

"They're looking for a forger for their network." I conceal my surprise.

"You're one of those who are revolted by torture, so I mentioned your name..." Henri goes on.

"But I haven't made any forged papers for years, as you very well know, Henri."

"I know that like me you think this war's absurd. Think about it and tell me yes or no."

"Who are these Algerians who've contacted you?'

"The MNA."[3]

Stirring my coffee, I look at Henri for a moment. The MNA, the first party supporting Algerian independence led by Messali Hadj, refuses to work together with the FLN. The two are in fact aging a bloody fratricidal war against each other.

"They've got the men, the structures, it's a very large network," he adds.

"Okay then, so what do they need exactly?"

"They want a hundred French identity cards. They can pay. Ten million francs.[4] So, is it yes or no?"

3. Mouvement national algérien (Algerian National Movement). [MM]

4. Old francs. The 'new franc' was introduced in 1960, and had the face value of one hundredth of the old franc, but people continued to talk in old francs for many years after. The offer would actually have been for 100,000 (new) francs. [MM]

"I need time to think it over," I eventually reply.

"OK, I'll tell them. In a week, same time, same place." Henri tears a page from his diary in two and gives me one half. "Someone will have the other half. He's the one you'll give your answer to."

I slip the torn piece of paper in my pocket, say goodbye to Henri, leave the café and plunge into the gray fog in the city. There's nothing like a quick walk along the embankment for thinking something over. What exactly is all this about? If the MNA needs identity cards, why not make them for them? I've seen in the past that it's possible to work for different groups at the same time, as long as they're fighting for the same goal. During the Resistance I didn't concern myself with whether the requests came from the FTP, the MOI or the MLN. Today I'm independent, therefore free... Nevertheless there are two serious questions that bother me, the first being the armed struggle between the MNA and the FLN. The second is the money. Ten million for a hundred cards—it isn't the amount that shocks me. You need finance to be able to produce forgeries; they cost a lot in time, equipment and materials. But being offered a specific sum in advance takes me directly to the question of the ethics. I'll have to speak to Jeanson about it before coming to a decision, and it so happens that I'll be seeing him tomorrow at Marcelline's to give him an update on the requests in progress.

One week later Philippe calls me: "Adolphe, come over, I have to talk to you," he demands imperiously.

I immediately dash over to his apartment, concerned that something serious might have happened between the Algerian and him. A disagreement, an argument or worse... Philippe opens the door, exclaiming, "Oh, Adolphe! Your Algerian, he was a very cultured man. Basically, what he's doing is resistance, as we were. If you have any more like that, you can send them to me."

I can't help smiling at the idea of this amazing pair living under the same roof. They talked about classical music, literature and philosophy, then about their struggles and the racism of which both their nations are victims.

Time moves on. I put my hand in my pocket to check that the torn diary page Henri gave me the previous week is still there, and I thank Philippe once again for his hospitality before setting off for the *Saint-Claude* to meet the representative of the MNA, who'll be waiting for my reply to their request for a hundred French identity cards.

"Just watch out, the MNA's in cahoots with the cops," Francis said to me after making some inquiries.

I sit down away from the other customers, at the same table where I sat with Henri in a corner of the back room, away from eavesdroppers. A man of around forty, looking like John Q. Public, comes over and sits down at the table. He takes his half diary page out of his pocket and hands it to me. I give him mine. He has sad, protruding eyes, a heavy, round face that doesn't match his small hands, which are spidery, as if they didn't belong to him. A policeman? Perhaps. Perhaps not. We wait a while before speaking. He looks at me, I look at him. Finally I'm the one who breaks the silence: "Listen, I've given your proposition a long, hard thought, and I'm not going to undertake the work."

He frowns and for a moment a look of disappointment crosses his face. I put on an embarrassed expression before I continue, pretending to be sincerely sorry.

142

"You know my history. You know what I did during the Resistance, don't you?"

"Yes."

"You will also know that I'm Jewish... It's not that I'm racist... But after all they are Arabs..."

The man nods. Apparently he can understand me.

11

JUNE 1961. When I was going home a few days ago I saw a man who seemed to be waiting outside the building. I felt his look and dress were characteristic of a policeman. The way he was waiting was too natural. His gray raincoat, his sharp, sly look, like a fox. I made an about-turn before he spotted me. I went for a walk. I went to have a coffee. When I came back, he was still there. I immediately left again. The film of Françoise Sagan's novel *Aimez-vous Brahms?* with Ingrid Bergman, Yves Montand and Anthony Perkins was on at the Grand Rex. I disappeared into the queue and into the dark auditorium, finally going back home much later. That time the man wasn't there anymore. Paranoia? I doubt it. After the wave of arrests the previous year, no detail is to be taken lightly. Almost all the agents of the Jeanson network are behind bars. As for the others, they managed to disappear while there was still time. Jeanson himself, his right-hand man Daniel and a few others whose cover had really been blown, fled using forged documents. They went to the Belgian support network of the FLN and continued their activities from outside France. Since then, the French network has been operating under the aegis of Henri Curiel's organization, but last October Curiel was also captured by the police and thus finally met the hundreds of FLN militants languishing in Fresnes Prison.

There aren't many of us still operating in the old organization. If I escaped being arrested, it wasn't by a miracle. It wasn't easy, but I managed to get it accepted that people couldn't just turn up at the laboratory. I insisted I only have one contact, although that wasn't aways respected, and I made every effort to keep out of the life of the network. But this time I smell trouble. Sometimes you have to anticipate disasters; if I stay here the noose will eventually tighten around my neck. The man at the bottom of the building isn't the only sign. It's quite possible that the surveillance has gotten as far as me, for during the trial I couldn't avoid Roland Dumas—who was defending the French accused—coming to see me repeatedly, nor Francis Jeanson who would also come, in disguise, when he was a wanted man. And that's not counting the fact that all the media fuss over the trial, the manifesto of the 121 and the arrest of Georges Arnaud, imprisoned for having done an exclusive interview with Francis Jeanson while he was on the run, had caused a lot of commotion and rallied numerous people to our cause. New members had been recruited, young ones to take the place of the former agents, and not all of them, put forward by sponsors, had had the time to be trained in the nuts and bolts of a clandestine existence. Information had been exchanged on the phone, precautionary measures and codes hadn't been observed.

Following the visit of the suspicious man in the gray raincoat, I immediately sounded the alert. The decision of the leadership in Brussels was unanimous and categorical: the risk of the laboratory being discovered must be avoided at all cost. The next day, I leave Paris in total secrecy. This time I have to go underground, and that means the end of my independence. The laboratory of forged documents is going to be moved to Brussels, from now on I'm going to be paid a regular 'allowance', as are other members of the network, and the organization will take care of all the production expenses. For the last few days, organizing my escape has been like a marathon. A thousand things to think about, to arrange. First of all to solve the 'Spanish problem'. José, Carlos and Juan, three anti-Franco Spanish republicans whom I've been helping for several years now alongside my other work, have just come for each to collect a 'box' containing rubber stamps, inks, a metal with a very low melting point to make relief stamps and a few tools that ought to let them continue without me during my absence.

I also had a large stock of blank documents to make before I left in order to deal with emergencies while I'm reinstalling an operational laboratory in Belgium. The press had been rolling without interruption for a week.

The preparations for my departure were almost finished. I was getting ready to go out to see my two children, Serge and Marthe, aged ten and eleven, who lived with their mother, when Jeannette, my liaison agent, came rushing into the laboratory, desperate for a key to open a Zenith lock. I gave her a dozen keys explaining, however, that the Zenith was a security lock and none of them was going to work. She wouldn't listen and, after having made me promise to wait for her, dashed off as quickly as she came.

One hour later Jeannette was back. As I'd predicted, the keys hadn't worked. She sank into one of the big armchairs in the waiting room, her head in her hands, and gave a long sigh.

"You're not going to tell me what's happened?"

"You have to help me, Joseph. One of the heads of an FLN section has just been arrested along with his partner, a Frenchwoman who's a CGT union official, in their apartment in Paris. Fortunately the cops didn't find anything at their place. But she has another apartment, in her own name, and that's where they keep the section's archives. If the cops discover the address, they'll have the names of hundreds of FLN militants who're in danger of being sent to prison, or being shot by the OAS if the police reveal their names. The keys don't work, and we can't break the door down without someone noticing. I just don't know what to do now."

It was the first time I'd seen Jeannette in such a panic. She was a young woman of twenty-four, a graduate of the IDHEC[1] working as an editor for the film review *Positif,* who'd become my liaison agent over a year ago when all my former contacts from the older generation had had to go into exile. I'd immediately seen that Jeannette was the kind of woman who wasn't fazed by anything. Her fears? She'd suppressed them since the day when, snuggled up in her mother's arms in a group following a guide who was leading them across the border, she'd crossed the demarcation line between the Occupied Zone and the Free Zone. A German soldier had appeared and led all the families away—apart from her and her mother, who in desperation had plunged into the bushes. The memory of that experience and of the stones people had thrown at her sister with insulting cries of 'Yid!' had left her keenly sensitive to the sting of racism and with an insatiable need to fight against injustice and the idea that commitment has to be total and absolute. She and I were birds of a feather.

"Her name is Madame François and her door's on the third floor, on the right," Jeannette had murmured as she scribbled the address on a scrap of paper. Then, before dashing down the stairs on another mission, she'd whispered, "Thanks, Jo. I'll repay you for this some day."

Since then, I've been practicing the use of the crow bar. I didn't

1. Institut des hautes études cinématographiques—Institute of Advanced Film Studies.

have too much difficulty forcing the door of the laboratory bath-room but I left great nasty marks on the wood. I'll have to find a way of going about it more cleanly before I tackle the kitchen door. With a thin metal plate stuck between the crow bar and the door perhaps. I have a try and, with a violent shoulder-thrust, the door gives way without a scratch on it.

After having forced two more doors for practice, I take a blank French ID card I have ready. I type in the details: Surname: François, First Name: Julien. That way I can pretend to be her brother. I trim my beard carefully, then go to the photographic studio to take a self-portrait that I develop in passport format. I stick in the revenue stamp, stamp the card then dilapidate and age it a bit so that it doesn't look too new. It's already nine o'clock, and the sun is just setting. What do I look like? A burglar? It's better to go about it openly so as not to arouse suspicion. I'll do it tomorrow morning, before taking the train to Brussels, especially since I've got my own things to stash away. I place all the compromising items from the lab—photoengraving plates, documents of all nations, revenue stamps, rubber stamps—in a large case and put that in the trunk of a car I've borrowed from a woman friend a few hours before. If the police arrest me in Madame François' apartment, they won't find anything at my place. It's better if they assume they're dealing with a bag-carrier rather than the FLN forger. I'll park the Citroen not very far away, somewhere near Rue du Louvre, and tell my friend where it is. If she still hasn't heard from me by the next evening, she'll collect the contents of the case and give them to Marie-Aline, who'll know what to do with them.

In the morning I go down to the bistro at eight for my coffee. Leaning on the bar, I catch the conversation between the owner and a weary old alcoholic.

"Have you seen that? They've pulled in another o' those FLN bitches."

The owner waves his newspaper in the customer's face, who nods apathetically. I ask if I can have a look. It's on the front page of *France Soir.* A big photo of Madame François and her partner, one of the FLN officials for the Paris region. It's already made the papers—I don't have a minute to lose. I pay for my coffee and run up the stairs to the laboratory four at a time. Two minutes later I leave, wearing gloves, carrying a large suitcase and jump into the first taxi.

When I get there, a small apartment block in a public housing project in Aubervilliers, it's impossible to avoid the concierge's desk. She is sure to have read the paper. It's better to go and announce myself.

"Good morning. I'm Julien François, the brother of Madame François on the third floor."

In order to win her trust, I show her my ID. Since she doesn't react either way, I question her, just to see. Whether she decides to call the police or not, at least I'll know where I stand and how much time I'll have to get the job done.

"You've heard about my sister?"

She stares at me, curious. "No. Has something happened to her?"

"Yes. Hasn't anyone told you?"

"As you can see, no one has. What is it?"

"She's been hospitalized with paratyphoid fever. She's asked me to get her a few things, and I haven't got the keys. I wanted to tell you that I'm going to open the door and change the lock."

"Oh, right. Yes, go ahead. And how's your mother?"

"Oh, you know. Getting older."

I go up to the third floor and locate the door. It gives way as

149

soon as I put pressure on the crow bar. I enter a dark room with the shutters closed. I press the light switch, but it doesn't work. The indicator on the electricity meter is pointing to zero. Strange. It's probably booby-trapped; I don't touch it. Getting it going again might set off a warning system in the police station on the corner, and I'd find a reception committee at the entrance to the building. Anyway, I've brought a flashlight with me.

First of all I replace the lock. Then I have a quick look around the apartment. The big kitchen cabinet Jeannette told me about is right in front of me. That's where the archives are kept, but it won't open; it's locked.

Once more I force the lock. I switch on my flashlight; there are heaps of files, stacked next to each other. I flick through one. Names of activists, their addresses, the amount of their dues. In another, reports on incidents and missions with the names of those involved at every level of the hierarchy. Then another... A list of the names of Algerians the FLN has ordered to join the *harkis*, the Algerian soldiers loyal to the French. A shiver runs down my spine. Documents, reports, accounts, correspondence, file after file, it's the whole life of the section spread out before me. I have to be quick. If the police get their hands on this there'll be a real massacre.

I stuff all the documents into a suitcase any which way and get ready to leave, but suddenly I stop, as if paralyzed by a premonition. What if there's other incriminating evidence in other places about the apartment?

To be sure, I go through the whole apartment. I discover more files in a cupboard nearby. Then, in the toilet, several garbage bags with bundles of documents torn in four, therefore very easy to put back together. It's a disaster. Impossible to take away all that quantity of paper in one shot. I have no choice—I'll have to sort them out, only keeping the most important documents, those with names, photos, important details. I don't touch the radio sets and the rifle I find in the cupboard. No time, no space. I double-lock the door when I leave and, carrying my heavy suitcase, go back down the stairs. At the bottom I meet the concierge again and slip her a bill. Not too much, not too little.

"I'll just take her this valise for the moment and don't be surprised if you see my nephew tomorrow. I'll send him to do a little housework. When everything's cleaned up he'll give you the new keys."

Jeannette had asked me to hand the archives over to Livio, at midday, in the *Terminus Nord* brasserie opposite the station. Because I've had to make a selection of the documents, I'm an hour and a half late. Livio's waiting for me, nervous, his face white with anxiety.

I sit down and slip the suitcase under the table. "There's the stuff."

"I can't take it," he replies, pushing it back to me with his foot.

"Why?"

"I'm an official of the Association of Algerian students. They've got a file on me."

"Well that wasn't in the plan... OK, I'll deal with the suitcase. But there's still lots of stuff left in the apartment. Documents, a rifle, radios."

"I can send a man."

"Here're the keys."

As I leave with the suitcase, I'm doubly vigilant. A glance at my watch. My train for Belgium has just left.

12

AFTER SEVEN YEARS of the struggle for independence, and at a time when the OAS bombs were exploding every day, when there was no end to the massacres and torture in the remote hills of Algeria, when the peaceful demonstration of October 17, 1961 turned into a bloody tragedy[1] and the hunger strikes in Fresnes started again,[2] with more and more prisoners taking part, responsibility for supplying the network with forged papers at the Rue de la Loi laboratory in Brussels now fell, under my supervision, to Gloria de Herrera, known as 'Katia' for, as well as the photoengraving and printing of papers, I now had a quite different mission to carry out. To inundate France with forged banknotes and thus destabilize the economy if the government persisted in its refusal to open negotiations—the idea was far from new. In short: economic blackmail. More radical action to

1. In a crackdown ordered by police chief Maurice Papon, Paris police turned their guns on 30,000 pro-FLN protesters gathered by the Seine. The exact number of casualties remains in dispute as Papon directed records to be destroyed. In 1998, Papon was sentenced to ten years' imprisonment for crimes against humanity because of his collaboration to deport at least 1500 French Jews to Nazi death camps. [MM]

2. Some four thousand Algerian nationals held in French prisons went on a nineteen-day hunger strike in November 1961 to protest being locked up as common criminals when the government had clearly arrested them for political reasons. The strike was halted after assurances by The Red Cross that they would be given a different regimen, but then continued when demands were not met. *The New York Times* reported on November 20, 1961: "Mohammed Ben Bella and four other Algerian rebel ministers held by the French since 1956 have sworn to continue their hunger strike until liberated and permitted to participate in the Algerian peace talks." [MM]

speed up the end of hostilities. But if it was to be taken seriously, it had to be credible. Put into action.

There had already been one attempt. Pablo, the leader of the 4th International, had gathered several experienced printers together in the Netherlands, but what he couldn't know was that one of them had been tailed by an agent of the Netherlands secret services. They had just started printing forged banknotes when the police arrested them.

This time there was no question of playing the apprentice sorcerer by working with just anyone. True, my laboratory couldn't print as quickly as a national mint, but all the same, in one week I'd managed to fill a single cardboard box with notes of 100 francs in the laboratory storeroom. Only Daniel, Omar and Katia were in on it. We hadn't settled on a final amount. I would keep on printing as long as there was no end to the war—that was the plan.

The start of my new life in Belgium had been a very emotional business. Because of having to clear out Madame François' apartment, I'd arrived in Brussels twenty-four hours late. I'd ended up hiding the suitcase with the archives and other compromising material in the attic closet above the photographic studio and asking Marie-Aline to arrange for them to be sent on to me. So I'd got on the train at the agreed time but a day later, heartbroken at the fact that I hadn't been able to find the time to give my children a goodbye kiss.

When I got to the furnished apartment where we were to meet in Brussels, I was no longer expected. There I found Omar Boudaoud, the chairman of the federal committee of the French Federation of the FLN, who'd been leading the organization since 1957 and whom I now met for the first time. Then there was Jeannette, sobbing inconsolably at the thought that I might have been arrested because of her, and Katia, who was soon to become my right-hand woman, and my partner as well. My appearance, as if by a miracle, was greeted with an immense sigh of relief, as if I'd suddenly come back to life and, with me, the hundreds of FLN militants whose names were on the documents in the archives.

The pleasure Omar and I both felt at our meeting wasn't feigned. I'd often heard Omar's leadership qualities praised, and I was pleased to discover that he matched up to his reputation. He had the stature of a great leader, radiating serenity, intelligence and swift judgment. My past in the Resistance, my experience of clandestine work and my commitment, as a Jew, to the Algerians particularly commanded his respect.

For several weeks I'd been working on the idea of trying the forged banknotes plan again. Once we were alone together I put forward the project to him. Omar wasn't very enthusiastic, especially after the Dutch fiasco. Though it was true that the operation had failed, I felt that the idea itself was a good one and certainly worth considering. I told Omar what I felt about this interminable war. If it were to go on for years to come, given the way the hatred was growing on either side of the Mediterranean we'd soon have to finally abandon any hope of Franco-Algerian friendship. I had the feeling that everything we could do had already been tried: armed struggle, diplomatic negotiations, intellectual propaganda, political argument, the insubordination of the young soldiers, and I was afraid that the OAS assassinations would provoke similarly violent responses. It was due to the intervention of our network, in particular the arguments put forward by Francis Jeanson, that it had been possible to avoid the war spreading to French soil. At one time, in 1958, the French federation of the FLN had been preparing a series of attacks on the French mainland as a response to four years of war. Francis had managed to persuade Omar to restrict the attacks to military, police and industrial targets. As a pacifist, I saw the 'forged notes' project as an excellent way of applying pressure without getting caught up in a spiral of violence. I knew that seven long years of conflict had not been without effect on the state coffers. Would the government take the risk of seeing the economy, which was already shaky, weaken even more? Eventually Omar had no objection and we decided to launch the operation, while still making forged documents our priority, of course.

Belgium was a hub for border crossings. Belgian laws only required foreigners to register after three months' residence, so every three months we had to move to different premises and change our identities, which meant we never needed to register with the police. Lots of decisions were made there, at the top level. The five members of the federation management committee— Omar Boudaoud, the boss; Kaddour Ladlani, in charge of administration; Ali Haroun, press and information; Saïd Bouaziz, head of the armed section known as the Special Organization (OS); Abdelkrim Souici, treasurer—used to travel through Belgium at least once a month, but frequently much more often.

Thus it wasn't sheer chance that many former members of the Jeanson network had been hiding there for several years. The struggle could still be pursued from Belgium. Daniel, Francis' assistant, had never given up his responsibility for the escape routes. Replaced in France by Curiel's right-hand man, he now looked after all the crossings of international borders. The Belgian network was perfectly organized with women and men whose courage was incontestable, guides mostly who would cross the Belgian, French, German, Swiss and Italian borders, and never complained when I had to wake them up at four in the morning to give them the necessary documents for an urgent mission. At the police level, Belgium gave the impression of absolute calm compared with Papon's police in France. I never had the feeling I was being followed. But the calm was deceptive: when you opened the door of your car, when a package was delivered, you had to beware of bombs. The bloody attacks of the OAS went well beyond the French borders.

Once I was there I had to set up everything from scratch, without wasting any time at all. From the start it had been agreed that Katia would assist me, for she was a surrealist painter and had been trained as a restorer of works of art. An American and a committed communist who had been very much involved in the Jeanson network from the very beginning, she had fled McCarthyism on the same ship as her friends Man Ray and André Breton. She was the one who looked for premises for me before I arrived, and found them with a couple belonging to the Belgian network who lived with their children in a large apartment, of which they allowed us to use one room. We would arrive in the morning, after they'd gone out, and leave in the evening before they returned. I managed to set up a fully equipped, functioning laboratory in the room within two days. I bought a little enlarger, then turned it into a copier to make the templates. I had the network buy me a hand press, a tiny thing compared with my huge 'litho' in Rue des Jeûneurs on which I printed the documents, though one by one. I made photosensitive plates for printing flat and in relief. My centrifuge was no longer made out of a bicycle wheel, as it had been during the Resistance, but out of an electric 78-rpm record player after I'd tinkered with the internal drive-belt so that I could vary the speed.

Very soon we had to move again. A comrade in the network rented a large place for us in Rue de la Loi—the address, as I discovered much later, of the Belgian outpost of the Red Orchestra[3]—and we could start printing forged banknotes.

The ones I chose were those of a hundred new francs; that was a sufficiently substantial amount. I had to study the structure of the paper, its weight, its rigidity, the noise it made when you shook it to make it crackle, its texture to the touch. By chance, going through the stock of a wholesaler I found some paper that seemed very close. All I had to do was to color it very slightly, with a dying process using alcohol so that the paper wouldn't swell too much while it was being soaked, to make it identical to the paper banknotes were printed on.

Then, with a special rolling press of my own invention, set very tight, I smoothed and finished off the paper. Napoleon was on it in his bottle-green jacket with yellow stripes and crimson collar, his gaze fixed on the Arc de Triomphe. The black ink of the numbering was slightly raised. The outlines were full of ornamentation and complicated flourishes, rosettes and sprays of flowers interwoven and with important variations in the color. The choice of inks and dyes needed gave me a real headache. Finally I analyzed the watermarks of higher and lower density. There were also some in color. After several weeks of analysis and tests I finally made some trials that were conclusive. And, gradually, the banknotes started to pile up in the laboratory storeroom. First a small cardboard box full. Then two, then three...

It was the end of the afternoon on a very ordinary day. Katia was yawning and rubbing her eyes. There was one photo left to

3. The Russian anti-Nazi spy network organized by Léopold Trepper during the Second World War.

attach to a driver's license before going home. We hadn't had much sleep the previous night because of a last-minute urgent request. Daniel had knocked on our door late in the evening asking for two ID cards and two driver's licenses that Cécile Marion, alias 'Maria', was to take to the French border in the middle of the night, using the route through the forest. So I'd gone back to the lab at that late hour; Katia came with me because she didn't want to stay by herself. Once we'd made the documents, we delivered them to Maria. She'd fallen asleep while waiting and greeted us with her eyes gummed up with sleep, though still smiling as always. For five years now Maria had spared no effort to help us. Since she was blonde, with angelic looks and could go anywhere, the organization relied on her for lots of liaison work. She still had to wait more than an hour, until three in the morning, before setting off, and we suggested we should stay there to help her stay awake.

Katia lit herself a cigarette and sighed as I closed the last eyelet of the photo on the identity card.

"I'll wait outside, I need some fresh air," she said, putting on her coat.

Before turning off all the lights, I opened the door of the storeroom as I did every evening, to have a quick look at my output, which was growing. More than a square meter of boxes full of tightly packed banknotes of a hundred new francs. How much could it amount to? Frankly I had no idea; I never bothered to count. I locked the door before going out. Every evening we used to walk home to enjoy what was left of the daylight. Only a few days previously we'd changed our identities and moved house for the fourth time, as demanded by our clandestine existence in Belgium. Our new home, a furnished apartment of no particular attraction, had a nice view over the Sablons district. No sooner

158

had we gotten back than Katia automatically switched on the radio, then hung her jacket and bag on the coat-rack and was about to slump onto the sofa and light a cigarette, when she suddenly froze and held her breath. The radio was blaring full blast. "A historic day," the journalist kept repeating. The Évian Accords and just been signed. It was March 18, 1962—the cease-fire had just been announced. Algeria was independent. The fruit of so many years of effort. Katia fixed her eyes on me in a look full of peace and relief. Around us the city was calm, almost completely still. No outbursts of joy, not even whoops of jubilation from the North African women. Brussels was not celebrating Algeria's independence.

There was no celebration in our new home either, but we were happy.

My immediate reaction was to rush over to the telephone and call Jeannine, my ex-wife, so I could talk to my children. How long had I been waiting for this moment! It had been almost two years since I'd seen them. I was trembling as I dialed the number. Jeannine picked up the receiver; I could hear the voices and laughter of Marthe and Serge, who were playing close by, right next to my ear. After I'd gone through a long explanation and asked her if she'd be kind enough to send the children to me by train, Jeannine said something I'll always remember: "We thought you were dead, Adolphe, but I always knew that if you weren't, you were sure to be doing something good."

"And the money, what did you do with that?"

What d'you think? We burnt it. The idea of doing anything else with it never crossed our minds. And then, as you can well imagine, I wasn't stupid enough to number the notes. We were determined to put them in circulation—if the war continued—and in that case I'd have numbered them. But, despite everything, I was hoping it would never come to that and that the conflict would find a diplomatic solution we could be more proud of.

Questions of money inevitably cause big problems. It's always with money that the troubles begin. I trusted Katia absolutely, of course, and she was the only one who knew where the forged banknotes were kept. But information could have slipped out, someone could have heard us talking, have figured out what we were doing. Money arouses cupidity, and by its very nature has the power to affect commitment and corrupt the minds of those you thought most honest. Numbering them too soon could have been like signing my own death warrant. When we started the forged money project, several things happened that put me on my guard. The behavior of some people around me changed from one day to the next. For example, I remember a woman in the network suddenly starting to make advances toward me when we'd known each other for four years already and there'd never been anything of that kind between us before. It's wearying to be suspicious of everyone and everything. I wasn't unhappy to see the money go. I'd be able to relax again.

Don't imagine burning banknotes is a simple matter. It's true that they catch fire easily, but they can also blow away. It took us almost a month to get it done. There was so much of it. With Katia's help, I dug a hole in the garden of a Belgian friend in the network, so that I could destroy it in small batches day by day. A bonfire that seemed interminable to us. I was watching almost a year's work go up in smoke. I enjoyed that, watching the banknotes burn. I was exultant, drunk at finding peace again.

13

I CAME BACK TO FRANCE in the course of the summer of 1963, exactly one year after the cease-fire in Algeria. The war was over, but that didn't mean my work was finished. We still had to ensure the security of the leaders and the members of the network who had remained underground, allow them to cross the borders in the other direction, organize their return and then liquidate everything—premises, apartments, vehicles—burn compromising material, obliterate every last trace of our illegal activities. It had taken a whole year to get that done.

I knew that a lot of the former members of the network had gone to Algeria to take part in the reconstruction of the country, but for the moment there was no reason for me to join them. I'd done what I had to do, Algeria was independent and I considered that the politics of the country were no business of mine, especially since I'd been totally taken aback by the fratricidal conflict between the former leaders of the revolution in the race for power. Once the anti-colonial struggle had been won, they made war among themselves. Worse still, I'd been profoundly shocked by the fate of the *harkis*. I was furious at the attitude of the Algerian government, which allowed the massacres to take place, but even more at the absolutely immoral stance of the French government that had been cowardly enough to simply abandon them there and then, when they knew full well what fate awaited them.

Katia also wanted to go back to France. We borrowed a car from a friend in the Belgian network and crossed the frontier clandestinely. To be honest, there wouldn't have been any risk in my traveling under my real name, but I'd fled the country to live an illegal existence, and my personal documents were still hidden in the Rue des Jeûneurs laboratory. For Katia, on the other hand, the situation was even more complicated, since there was still a conviction hanging over her head like the sword of Damocles. When the Jeanson network had been broken up she ought, like all the others, to have been imprisoned awaiting trial but, thanks to her American nationality, she'd been temporarily released. Being under no illusion as to the likely verdict and sentence, we'd decided, together with Francis Jeanson, to get her out of the country immediately to Belgium via Switzerland and Germany. She'd crossed the borders with forged papers and wearing various wigs, since her photograph had been on the front page of the newspapers, notably in an article with the headline: "These are the Parisian Women of the FLN,"[1] which described her as the network's recruiting officer. Convicted in her absence, she was the only one of the women who'd been arrested who had managed to avoid ending up in Petite Roquette Prison.

I went back to the lab in Rue des Jeûneurs. I had continued to pay the rent through Marie-Aline, and M. Petit had profited from my prolonged absence by setting up an office in what had been my dining room. Seeing me return, he was afraid I'd insist that he

1. *Paris-Presse*, February 1960.

leave. In fact the opposite was the case. The premises were spacious enough to allow him to stay, and I was both surprised and delighted to find that he'd been there to see that everything was kept in good order. I reactivated my firm, went back to being a photographer, found my boxes with their precious contents still intact. Katia and I moved into a small apartment, and I told my family, friends and clients that I was back.

There were two stories going around to explain my disappearance. Those who had been involved in the operation knew the truth. The others thought I'd gone to work for Agfa in Germany after I'd broken up with Marie-Aline, preferring to get away from Paris to give me time to forget her.

The weather was fine, it was summer. Paris, deserted by all those who went away on vacation, was quiet and left with its picture-postcard views. Fashion favored the urchin cut for girls and colorful trousers for the boys. The war, all the worries were behind us. I was glad to be back, to wander around the sunny streets, the embankments and the gardens, to immortalize the peaceful weeks with my camera.

But Katia was in a bad way. She was suffering from what I called the 'depression of the ex-combatant', the profound malaise to which I was unfortunately no stranger myself, since I too had been through it at the conclusion of every struggle. A clandestine period leaves indelible traces. It makes a deep impression on you and cannot simply be brushed away. When you've learned to live with fear, risked your life, your freedom, experienced dangerous and romantic adventures, always under pressure and dedicating your life to a cause you've decided is pure, becoming reintegrated in society can be a painful ordeal.

Katia found she couldn't paint anymore nor feel emotion or be satisfied with simple things. She felt alone, useless. The euphoria mingled with fear, which is so characteristic in the underground, had vanished. Daily life seemed terribly insipid and futile. She was overwhelmed by melancholy.

It was no use my fussing over her, making every effort to think up things to comfort her, to cheer her up; nothing I could do or say made her feel any better.

In spite of our love, she couldn't forget that Véra, her former lover, was still imprisoned in La Roquette and, given that her own situation was irregular, going to visit her was clearly out of the question.

She wouldn't go out at all, refusing to be seen in her apathetic state, declined repeated invitations from her old friends, no longer went to the places where the surrealist painters used to meet. Determined to bear the burden of her melancholy alone, Katia drowned her torment deep in the whisky bottle; she couldn't get to sleep until she'd drained it to the last drop.

I could understand her, but at the same time I realized my presence was no help to her. So I decided to shut myself away too, only in my laboratory. Work would be my therapy. I had projects for the future, personal ones this time. I intended to develop my own photos, the thousands of shots I'd taken since the Liberation. I planned to exhibit my works and to become—why not?—the artist my political commitment had never allowed me to be. My boxes were full of magnificent photos that were just waiting to be brought out. And then I was thirty-eight. My friends were beginning to make a name for themselves, each in his own field. Until then I'd never thought of a career; now I decided it was time.

But no sooner had I gotten back than the anti-Franco Spaniards, alerted to my return by mutual friends, came to see me.

I'd already thought my past might catch up with me but had never imagined the respite would be so brief. I'd given some of their people a crash course before I left, and I'd hoped that would mean they'd be completely self-sufficient by now. But it's not enough to be a good pupil to be a good forger. That means constant research because paper is changing all the time. Identity cards alone are not enough to allow someone to survive in the underground, which needs a whole pile of documents, from a driver's license to proof of one's address—say, a telephone or electricity bill.

Training courses had to be scheduled again and on a timetable that was pretty restrictive. José, the communist, Carlos, the Trotskyist and Juan, the anarchist, were all intelligent enough not to ask me where I'd been during the last two years, but because of their political differences they still refused to meet each other and work together. As far as I was concerned, I couldn't wait to get the training of my apprentices completed as soon as possible so that I would be left in peace and above all, of course, so that their efforts could help rid Spain of the unsavory Franco. But, first and foremost, I no longer wanted to sacrifice my own freedom. That, at any rate, was my state of mind when I made the acquaintance of an extraordinary man whose destiny I was to share from that day onward for years to come.

It was a mid-September afternoon. By what chance I couldn't say but—and this was very unusual—there were several clients visiting the laboratory at the same time, packed into the waiting room. The man in question was of medium height, broad-shouldered, slightly portly and with a huge black mustache, like the singer Georges Brassens. He'd been the first to arrive but no, he assured me, he wasn't in a hurry and he politely insisted I see all the others first. He took out his newspaper and waited patiently in an armchair in my anteroom.

When we were alone together he stood up and held out his hand. "I'm Stéphane," he said. "It's Jeannette who sent me. I'd like to talk to you."

That he should introduce himself with a first name would come from Jeannette, my former liaison agent, and that he straight away used the familiar '*tu*' indicated that he belonged to the FLN support networks. I locked all the doors so that we could discuss serious matters.

Let me give you a brief description. 'Stéphane', Georges Mattéi by his real name, was in his thirties. Of Corsican origin, he came from a communist family that was active in the FTP Resistance group; he'd done his military service in Algeria, where the army had 'taught him to kill', then, like the others of his generation, he'd been recalled in order to 'pacify' Algeria. A convinced anti-militarist, spotted as a leader during the demonstrations of the men who'd been recalled, because he'd chanted his wish for peace in Algeria louder than the others, the military hierarchy sent him with the other 'hard cases' to the Great Kabylia combat zone. He witnessed torture that he attempted to expose when he got back by publishing an article entitled *"Jours kabyles"* (Kabylian days) in *Les Temps modernes*.

A journalist, close to Sartre and Simone de Beauvoir, and with a strong belief in liberty and equality, in 1969 he took charge of the escape routes for bags with the Curiel network, after the Jeanson network had been broken down. The exceptional efficiency he showed meant that he became Henri Curiel's right-hand man until the ceasefire.

Mattéi and I exchanged views on Algeria. He'd gone over there in 1962, to see what it was like, but he'd felt no desire to settle down there as a *'Pied-rouge'*.[2] His opinion was that the reconstruction of Algeria was a matter for the Algerians and that to collaborate with them as a Frenchman gave him the unpleasant feeling of being part of a kind of disguised colonialism.

On many points we shared the same ideas, and we were concerned about the emergence of a current of religious fundamentalism. Despite everything, we were aware that a nation needed time to reconstruct its identity after a hundred and thirty years of colonization, and we were very hopeful about the future of the country.

He told me about the activities of the African liberation movements that now had their offices in Algiers and were supported by the Algerian government. From France, Curiel helped them through his organization, working in sympathy with them both legally and underground, and coordinating this was Stéphane's responsibility. Though he had accepted the task enthusiastically, Mattéi refused to become part of Curiel's group, on the one hand because he wanted to retain his independence, but also because of differences of opinion in political questions, especially after Curiel had come out in support of Ben Bella.[3] After that, relations between them had cooled, though without bringing their collaboration to an end.

Moreover, Mattéi wasn't focused on the African continent alone; he was equally concerned with promoting South American revolutionary struggles. During his first trip to Cuba in 1961 he'd made numerous contacts with South American revolutionary leaders, notably in Argentina, Venezuela, Brazil, Chile and the Dominican Republic.

I liked this man with the mustache. He wasn't pretentious,

2. 'Redfoot', the term for left-wingers who went to Algeria after independence, was used in opposition to the term *'pied-noir'* (blackfoot), meaning the French who had settled in Algeria. [MM]

3. An Algerian revolutionary who became the first president of Algeria. [MM]

didn't make a mystery of things or go on interminably about his activities. Not belonging to any political party, independent of all the networks—which reassured me all the more because, due to numerous unintentional pieces of carelessness, the support network for the FLN had broken all records for arrests—he was particularly distinguished by three qualities: he was serious, loyal and believed in universal human rights. He was so likable and had such a broad vision and extensive knowledge of international politics that we ended up talking until it got dark. Of course I was well aware he hadn't come to see me so that we could draw up a list of struggles for emancipation throughout the world, but he was polite enough not to rush things. It was only when it was getting late that he explained that he'd just come back from the Dominican Republic, which was going through a very serious political crisis. Hardly had the new democratic regime been established, following thirty years of a cruel dictatorship, than it was overturned by a military coup. The country was being torn apart by war. The leaders who were highest on the wanted list had had to flee. The revolutionaries were rushing to the mountainous bush to organize the armed struggle. The military promised to execute anyone who opposed the new dictatorship. In order to survive, to flee or to fight, they needed papers.

I agreed to help the Dominicans without hesitation, but I made it a point of honor to see that everything was clear between Stéphane and me, for there were a certain number of conditions that had to be respected. I insisted that I should have just one contact (himself), that I should be kept absolutely separate from the organization, and I warned him that I wouldn't accept a request from any intermediary or emissary, whoever he might be. Telephone contact was to be strictly avoided or at least kept to an absolute minimum. We would see each other at the laboratory. In order to avoid the risk of being arrested if the police should happen to have put a tap on the phone, any call to arrange a rendezvous in the town had to use a quarter-hour code to indicate an interval of three hours and one or two days: a rendezvous at midday meant three pm, at six pm meant nine o'clock; 'a quarter to' meant the preceding day; 'half past', two days after the stated date. In addition to that, if he should have a meeting with anyone in these networks, he must never come to see me on the same day. And then—this was the most important of my conditions—there was to be no question of money between us. I categorically refused to accept any payment and reserved the right to say yes or no to every request. If I were to have the least doubt about the merits of any request, I wouldn't carry out the work.

Since Mattéi also took the liberty of saying yes or no to those he was working for, I never had to say no to him.

Initially I'd assumed Mattéi would only call on my services occasionally, but I very quickly had to face up to the fact that I was wrong in that. People all over the world were fighting for their freedom. After the Dominicans and the Haitians, it was the Brazilians' turn to come under the yoke of a military dictatorship in 1964. Then, in 1966 following the Tricontinental Conference in Havana, during which the Latin American Solidarity Organization (LASO) was formed, Mattéi agreed to become the organizer of their clandestine support network for the revolutionary struggles operating from France. Under the aegis of LASO the revolutionary movements in Argentina, Venezuela, Salvador, Nicaragua, Colombia, Peru, Uruguay and Chile worked together for the revolution in Latin America, but in opposition to the Moscow line.

So gradually all these countries were added to my list, but that wasn't all since Mattéi, through the Curiel network, was also aiding the anti-apartheid movements in South Africa. Then there was Guinea, Guinea-Bissau and Angola, Portuguese colonies that were fighting for their independence. In 1967 Mattéi linked up with American pacifist groups refusing to serve in Vietnam. Since it was precisely because I didn't want to be part of the war in Indo-China that I'd left the French secret service, I could well understand them and immediately offered to supply forged papers to all American deserters who wanted them. I have to say that there were a lot of them.

Thus it was that in that year, 1967, I was supplying forged papers to combatants and draft-dodgers in fifteen different countries, and that was nothing compared with subsequent years, up to 1971.

It goes without saying that resuming my activity as a forger, especially at that rate, meant the end of my artistic ambitions. Refusing to be paid by the organizations, I had to find another way of making a living. Photographer by day, forger by night, my firm's accounts always in the red, I had a devil of a job doing the books at the end of the month. And my personal and family life was still in the same mess. Very often I couldn't keep my promise to take my children out for a walk on the weekend, and I could never explain what the reason was, even though I knew they'd waited hours for me. Since I had thousands of secrets I couldn't divulge, I spoke as little as possible to avoid inventing too many lies I might get tied up in. Katia, cured of her depression, had finally left. Later on I got to know Lia Lacombe, Peter Schaeffer's assistant at the ORTF,[4] with whom I moved into a new apartment on Rue Charles-Baudelaire. But, once again, my nocturnal activities meant I couldn't meet her expectations. My love life's always been full of

4. Office de radiodiffusion télévision française, the French state broadcasting service. [MM]

170

misunderstandings, but with Lia the situation reached the depths. I was working—she thought I was sleeping around. And since I had no way of putting her mind at rest, nor of letting her in on the secret, even if only to protect her, it was impossible to get the idea out of her head that I was in the arms of another woman while she was waiting for me until the small small hours, eyes brimming with tears and full of reproaches. I would tell her I was working on my exhibition, yet she never saw a single negative.

It's also true that when I was with her, my mind was often elsewhere. Though not where she imagined. I remember one day when my silence made her explode: "I've been talking to you for half an hour but you're just looking into space, you don't reply. Where *are* you?"

My reply was laconic: "In Angola."

"You've been seeing an Angolan woman?"

Scenes, arguments, tears and misunderstandings.

My secrets invariably led to this kind of problem. I never managed to reconcile my love life with my illegal activities, except when my partners were involved in the networks themselves. What's more, working day and night, I was always broke, I never took a holiday, I was never free. To be honest, I wasn't a good catch.

"You never thought of giving it all up?"

To tell you the truth, there were times when I was weary of all these sacrifices, weary of all the acrobatics I had to go through, of all the sleepless nights to pay the bills, of only sleeping in two-hour slots, of always being on the alert and checking that I wasn't being followed, of being unable to enjoy the company of my children, of making the women who loved me suffer—out of love—always imprisoned in the extreme solitude of my secrets. But I only had to think, even just for a second, of all the unknown men and women whose lives were in my hands, to immediately stop feeling sorry for myself. My love life, my career, my comfort and my pleasures were much less important than saving a life in danger— because the memory of the helping hand of the agents of the 6th section, who had saved me from certain death when I was being persecuted myself, was engraved on my memory forever.

Lia was sulking. It didn't make her any less beautiful. I'd just told her I was having to cancel the weekend in the country we'd planned. She switched on the radio "because of all this deafening silence between us," she moaned, though I think that above all she wanted news of the demonstrations. It was May 1968 and her son Pascal, about twenty, was taking part in them. The radio reported the confrontations. The young students were chanting poetic slogans while throwing cobblestones for sexual liberation, and that was great. The workers were setting up more and more pickets all around France, and that interested me even more.

The telephone rang. Lia was quicker getting to it than me: "It's for you. It's Stéphane," she said, visibly relieved that it wasn't a woman.

At the other end of the line Mattéi gave me a rendezvous for the next day at 8:45 in the evening at *La Rhumerie martiniquaise*, which in reality meant for this evening at six in *La Closerie des lilas*. I put on my coat and went out.

He ordered a beer and I, as usual, a white coffee. He wanted my opinion on a request that was a bit out of the normal.

"Tell me, what would you do for a guy who wants some forged papers to thumb his nose at the police, perhaps even hoping to be arrested?"

"Is his life in danger?"

"No. He got expelled from France because of the demos. He wants to come back to speak at a meeting where he's sure of being arrested again. He wants to make a media splash."

"What does he risk getting?"

"Expelled again, perhaps a short stay in the slammer; not very much, that is. Look, here's his latest photo. Of course he's dyed his hair brown for the occasion."

When I saw the photo, I smiled.

"So what do you think? Can you do it?"

I promised him the ID card for the next day. I had a big back-up of work, thus very little time to waste on something I wouldn't normally have considered an emergency, but in this case I felt like making an exception. I headed off to the lab and locked myself in the darkroom. It didn't take me long to make the ID card. I already had blank cards and rubber stamps ready, and sheets of revenue stamps. All that was left was to invent a typically French name, fill it in, attach the photo and make the card look used.

Three days later I went to pick up Lia at the ORTF to take her out to lunch. I'd been a bit hard on her recently. The café we'd chosen was particularly noisy. While most of those around us were talking about the demonstrations and the return of de Gaulle, Lia unbosomed herself of all her grievances about my conduct toward her: I never listened to her; I was never at home. I was quite happy to do as she wanted, to listen to her for as long as necessary, when my eye was caught by the photo in a newspaper a young blonde woman was reading. It was of Daniel Cohn-Bendit, now with brown hair, taken on the platform of the First of May movement. I couldn't help smiling.

Lia clicked her fingers right in front of my eyes to make me look at her: "You see, you're not listening to me."

"Oh, but I am, I am."

"You're looking at that blonde girl."

Of all the forgeries I made throughout my life, that was certainly the one that drew the most media attention and was the least useful, but I have to admit it was a great opportunity to thumb my nose at the strong-arm tactics of the authorities by demonstrating that there's nothing more porous than borders and that ideas have no respect for them.

In the end, making it possible for Cohn-Bendit to return clandestinely to France while he was banned from the country was my sole contribution to the May rebellion. On the one hand that was because, as a forger, I was always careful not to make my political views public, my place was not among the demonstrators but in my laboratory, where the requests continued to pour in; on the other because, even though I might physically be in Paris, my heart and mind were with those oppressed in the Third World. It was beyond the seas where I was most needed. And I did hope that the worldwide anti-authoritarian ferment of 1968 would breathe new life into the fight against inequality. It was in the context of all this upheaval that I saw Jeannette for the last time.

Jeannette and I had never lost sight of each other since she'd been my liaison agent in the Algerian war. Like Mattéi she'd taken a keen interest in the Cuban revolution. In 1963 she'd been making a documentary on the island, but the militant prevailed over the filmmaker and she abandoned the film to volunteer and join a group of guerrillas in Latin America. Eventually she joined the Guatemalan FAR (*Fuerzas Armadas Rebeldes*, Rebel Armed Forces). At first she traveled there a few times, then more and more often, always with forged documents I'd made.

The last time she came to the lab was to ask me for a new passport. She and her group were preparing something; they wanted to show that the death of Che Guevara wouldn't impede the progress of the revolution. I was concerned for her. I tried to dissuade her; at first I even refused to let her have the documents. She looked at me from the depths of her huge, melancholy eyes and, with her childlike smile, calmly replied that, forged papers or not, she was going anyway. So, very reluctantly, I complied with her request; and she flew off to Guatemala.

As usual, at the end of the summer, I didn't have any money to go away on holiday, and I continued my morning ritual: a large white coffee, a croissant and *Le Monde*, always in the same café.

The paper didn't give the name of the young Frenchwoman who'd shot herself through the mouth when the police knocked on her door, but I knew it was her. It could only be her.

How often had she played out the scene before me? It was something that kept cropping up in our conversations. How could she hold out if she were arrested, tortured? How could she refuse to speak? For Jeannette, only death could guarantee complete silence. She'd thought of a cyanide capsule; but then she'd have to hope it would work pretty quickly, otherwise they'd pump her stomach to bring her around. Shoot at the enemy in order to get herself shot? Too risky, she might just be wounded. No, Jeannette had HER solution and she demonstrated it to me several times. With her two outstretched fingers as the barrel of a revolver, she stuck them in her mouth, pointing slightly upward, "because against your temple there's a chance you might miss." She'd fire without hesitation, not even giving herself time to think about it.

I retched as I folded the paper. I couldn't get the croissant down. I put the money for the bill on the table and left without

175

even saying goodbye to the *patron*. I set off home but changed my mind when I realized it wasn't the best moment to run into Lia. Eventually I went to the laboratory.

I felt so guilty about allowing myself to be talked into giving her the passport that I locked myself in for two days and didn't open the door for anyone, didn't set foot in our apartment, didn't answer the phone; it even took me a great effort to get out of bed. It was no use telling myself she'd followed her ideals to the very end, that she would certainly not have wanted to die in any other way—I was too moved by her death to accept it rationally. And then it wasn't one of the most glorious periods of the revolution. There was still the Cuban example, of course, but what could one say about Fidel Castro and his alignment with Moscow? Everyone who came back from the island said that the time of celebration and hope was over. The watch kept on sexual morality, the restrictions on individual freedoms, the repression and the censorship were ominous signs. The model island was no longer as great as it had been. Since I would never see Jeannette again, since I found mourning difficult, I was suddenly overcome with doubt. Should I continue my activities, yes or no? Was it not time now to give it all up?

But only a few weeks later the Mexican demonstrations of 1968 ended in a bloodbath. In cold blood, the police fired on hundreds of students; the newspapers were talking of over three hundred deaths in a few hours and as many arrests. These events swept away all my doubts in one stroke. That was just the kind of thing I was fighting against.

The following week Mattéi came to the laboratory with a model Mexican passport to be copied in large numbers. Hundreds of wanted people had been forced to flee, and he was

176

already getting down to organizing the accommodation network. We were going to open wide the gates of Europe and freedom for them.

14

BY 1969 IT WAS SIX YEARS since I'd been making forged papers for Curiel's network and the OLAS countries through Mattéi, and I hardly need to add that a certain routine had been established. The requests came when they came, in little packages of ten, fifteen, sometimes a lot more, sometimes nothing for a while: identity cards, passports, driver's licenses, certificates, all kinds of documents—the daily round.

I was going through what you could call a calm period when, one summer's day, Annette Roger came knocking at the laboratory door together with one of her friends.

Annette and I had had a great rapport ever since the day when she'd persuaded me to meet Francis Jeanson. During the Algerian war she was one of the first victims of the wave of arrests that broke up the Jeanson network. Arrested along with the head of the FLN for the Marseilles region at the end of 1959, Annette was pregnant when she was locked up in Baumettes Prison awaiting trial. As she was a doctor, she took advantage of the complicity of some of the medical staff. A fellow doctor switched her tests and those of a patient who was seriously ill before submitting them to the specialist, who decided Annette should be temporarily released. Her trial had already begun, and she was well aware of what awaited her because the first verdicts of the Paris trials had just been returned, condemning her comrades to ten years in prison, and she made her escape doubled up in the trunk of a car, clutching her stomach to protect it from the jolts. She made it to Switzerland, then to Italy and finally Tunis, where she joined the Tunisian network of the FLN and became a psychiatrist for the Armée de libération nationale (ALN, National Liberation Army). Sentenced in her absence, she got ten years like the others. Once Algeria was independent, she was given very responsible posts in the Algerian Ministry of Health, where she worked for a number of years.

The last time she'd been to the laboratory, panting and in a hurry "between two urgent matters," the Soviet army had just invaded Czechoslovakia, putting a final end to "socialism with a human face" during the Prague Spring. She wanted to know if I was ready to help some of the reformers, who were in danger of being imprisoned and killed, to flee the country. Of course I said yes.

This time Annette's request was about the Greeks fighting against the dictatorship of the colonels. Jacqueline Verdeau, the woman who'd come with her, was asking for material aid for her resistance group in Greece. The coup d'état had taken place in 1967, and since then the regime had punished any kind of opposition severely. The rumors of censorship, persecution, imprisonment, deportation and torture were confirmed. Greece had recently been excluded from the Council of Europe, and numerous demonstrations of support and for the defense of human rights had been organized all over the world. I'd been astonished that for the last two years I had only had a small number of Greek documents to forge for the Curiel network.

"Until today we relied on a supply of forged documents from England, but they're no longer available," Jacqueline explained.

Jacqueline, a psychiatrist at Saint-Anne Hospital, was approaching forty and her smooth, round face immediately drew me to her. Nervously, she brushed back a lock of her fringe before going on: "It's become impossible to continue with any anti-government operations, and we're concerned about the safety of those on the wanted list."

Usually I didn't like to have too many different things on at once, nor to work for several organizations at the same time, but since it was only a matter of small quantities, I accepted.

The Greek ID cards were covered with a softer gelatin than the current plastic coating for documents. If you tried to take off the plastic cover to change the details on the card or attach a new photo, the entire board would come away with it. It was better to make the whole card from scratch. I'd already studied all the technical characteristics, so I could start as soon as she wanted. I agreed with Jacqueline that she would carry the ID cards in an ordinary woman's handbag that was big enough and in which I would sew two extra linings, a soft one with a stiff one underneath that would conceal the number of cards required. She would do as many return journeys to Athens as necessary, and we would proceed in the same way each time.

A few days later Jacqueline took off for Athens with six cards in the lining for a start. Precisely two days after Jacqueline left, I had an unexpected visit from Roland Dumas. He was accompanied by a law student. Stéphanie was very beautiful and she knew it. Silent, her hands stuck in the pockets of her jeans, she looked bored while Roland and I exchanged a few mutual memories. When she started to speak, her expression suddenly became animated. She talked quickly, in a clear, assured voice. Her comrades, a very active Greek resistance group, had commissioned her to find a forger as quickly as possible. Their usual supply route, in England, had just been cut off.

The principal task of Stéphanie's network was to organize escapes from the country through the Franco-Hellenic Association for Freedom in Greece, and their work had been halted in the same way as Jacqueline's by the arrest of the English forger. Stéphanie didn't just need ID cards but passports as well, and this time it wasn't just a matter of small quantities...

The following week it was the turn of Aurélie, Nathalie's babysitter from the time when I was living with Marie-Aline, to visit me. On the doorstep she ran into Mattéi, who had come to pass on a new request for Greek passports for Curiel. I felt genuine pleasure at seeing Aurélie again. The energetic woman with the flowing black mane standing before me completely swept away the image of the sad, timid adolescent I'd known ten years before. At the time Aurélie had told us she'd run away because of great family problems.

Marie-Aline and I took her under our wing, and I applied to be declared her legal guardian so that she wouldn't be sent back to the man who'd been beating her. The social services put her officially in my care.

Aurélie, who lived with me until she came of age, and even a little longer, during the years when I was making documents for the FLN, had eventually realized that it wasn't only photographs that were produced in the Rue des Jeûneurs lab. However, we never talked about it, and Aurélie kept out of it on her own initiative. Except for one evening when, seeing me about to collapse under the mass of work, she suggested she help me. It was the night before I made my escape to Belgium. We spent the whole night printing out the plates for Swiss documents that would be the network's reserve while the Brussels lab was being set up.

Aurélie was in great form. With roars of laugher she described her new life to me, happy to be able to tell me that she was working as a film editor for the cinema, which was what she'd always wanted to do. She was living with a man, Nicolas, whom she wanted to introduce to me but, snowed under with work as I was, I suggested we put the meeting off until the next month.

"But it's urgent!" she broke in.

For a moment I had the ridiculous notion that she wanted my support as an 'adoptive father', but Aurélie's urgent request was of a quite different nature.

Nicolas, the man she was living with, was a Greek revolutionary who'd come to Paris to study a few years previously and now divided his time between his work as a stage designer and the Greek Youth Resistance movement of which he was a passionate supporter. Nicolas, it seemed, had a favor to ask of me...

So that was how things around me were suddenly becoming hectic. All at once everyone wanted Greek documents. During the months that followed one client would leave the lab only for another to come in. I have to tell you that, as well as the Greek turmoil, I couldn't avoid having other friends, former members of the Jeanson network, coming to beg me to help them. Struggles were going on all over the world, and many of those who had supported the FLN felt, like me, that they owed a duty to the oppressed. It was a mad scramble; the knocking at my door was never-ending. For example there was the filmmaker, Mario Marret, for whom I supplied the film and necessary papers to make his documentary *Nossa Terra* in the bush of Guinea-Bissau with the rebels of the African Party for the Independence of Guinea and Cape Verde (APIGCV). I was already making forged papers for the APIGCV through Mattéi, but when Mario came to the laboratory again he brought with him the brother of Amílcar Cabral, the leader of the rebellion, a half-caste called Luís Cabral who in 1974, after the Carnation Revolution in Portugal and the death of Amílcar, would become the first president of Guinea-Bissau.

As he'd left the country illegally, Luís had to acquire new papers and find secure accommodation at once. I saw to everything, and that was the beginning of a long collaboration between us that was to make it possible for senior officials of the movement to travel around Europe. After Luís came João. And so on. I won't name them all—it would take too long—but while I'd been very careful all my life to avoid multiple contacts, within one year I found I'd ended up with more than a dozen clients at the same time.

Following the rule of keeping everything in separate watertight compartments, it was absolutely essential that no one should find out that I was working for other people—they should all believe they were 'the only one'—so, as far as humanly possible, I organized things so that they wouldn't meet each other. It still happened that I couldn't avoid two of them sitting in the waiting room at the same time, but I was sure each took the other for a normal client.

I had moved from an ordered routine to being run off my feet. Having multiple clients increased not only the amount of work but the risk as well. The least gesture, word, journey demanded extreme vigilance. I numbered the boxes with the orders then hid them among other, identical boxes containing photographic paper and proofs. The Dumas-Stéphanie box was no. 22, the Annette-Jacqueline box 78, the Aurélie-Nico box 43, etc.

Even though M. Petit, who arrived at nine in the morning every day and left at five, as regular as clockwork, never set foot outside his office, I now always kept my bundle of keys on me and made sure I locked the door of every room in the laboratory behind me. Since my clients weren't normal 'customers' and their requests not the kind of thing you write down in an order book, I had to put everything in code and retain it by memory—for when, for whom, how many—without ever getting mixed up.

Do I have to tell you that Lia had finally decided to break up with me? The separation took a long time and was full of sadness and misunderstandings, as our whole affair had been.

Once more permanently on the alert, I started to suffer from nervous fatigue. I made an assessment of the situation. I was one of the older generation, active in the area since the middle of the Second World War. And I was alone. There were numerous people fighting for freedom, but none, or almost none, in my field. Whenever necessary, I made forged papers for every life that was in danger, and the same question kept coming back to me: if it came to the point where I had to stop, if something should happen to me, who would take over?

I started to work on the project of who would replace me. Until this point I had taken the trouble, whenever possible, to train an apprentice in forging, rather than doing it myself. Often it wasn't necessary to make the whole document, it was enough for accomplices to steal or borrow passports on which only the photo had to be changed, or details such as the date, name, age. My training of people helped both to reinforce the autonomy of the networks and to lighten my load.

I was a very good teacher and had some excellent pupils. José Hipolito dos Santos, who was one of the leaders of the ULRA

(United League of Revolutionary Action), was a very assiduous pupil. He became an expert for military discharge certificates that allowed many young anti-colonialists to desert from the Portuguese army. Nicolas, Aurélie's boyfriend, had great manual aptitude and a resourcefulness that reminded me of myself. I know today that his talents as a forger saved many members of the Greek resistance. Either of them would have made a first-rate replacement, only they were both devoted to their movement, to *their* cause and not to causes in general. I suppose they had neither the time nor the desire to become 'professional' forgers.

We never went into the methods of making documents.

The African liberation movements that had their offices in Algiers often sent me new people to help out and to train. With caution I would either accept them or not, for I had to make a selection. It has to be said that at that time anyone demanding the liberation of this or that people, holding forth in any old way, with any old revolutionary terms, could hope for financial aid from Boumediene's government.[1] I arranged meetings in cafés well away from where I lived. I made inquiries, spent a long time assessing them, rejecting those who were talkative, inexperienced, proud, arrogant, hooligans…

I spent a long time observing and searching for the person who would be capable of taking over, both technically and morally.

"Did you find one?"

One of them could have been the right man. Fabrizio was in his thirties and had a good knowledge of printing. He really wanted to know everything and was interested in the struggles all over the world. I gave him some very intensive training. For six months he

1. Boumediene ruled Algeria through a revolutionary council after 1965 until his death in 1978. [MM]

spent two half days a week with me, and each time he left he took some practical work to do at home. He was smart, had a great memory and we progressed very quickly. I estimated that at that speed he would have completed his training in two years.

But little by little I detected attitudes, ways of talking that aroused my suspicions. Fabrizio had been sent by Solidarité, Henri Curiel's network, but as soon as we started to discuss it, he would criticize it in a singularly furious manner. It's true that not everyone was happy with Curiel's line. Better and better organized, the structure he'd put in place since the Algerian war was becoming much more effective and was expanding. As always in politics, the increasing power of a man or a group triggers off jealousy and rancor, disagreement and dissidence, hurt pride and the desire for a putsch.

But that wasn't what most concerned me about Fabrizio. In the course of the long discussions in which we got to know each other better, it was expressions such as 'more radical', 'to the very end', or 'if there's damage, so be it' that got me thinking. We were starting to hear about little groups of the extreme left, such as the Red Army Faction, the Baader-Meinhof gang or even the Red Brigades, whose bloody methods of urban guerrilla warfare I roundly condemned. For some time, many of the young people who joined the solidarity networks seemed motivated by the dubious desire to handle guns and money, idolizing the hooligans and forgetting the cause, slowly but inexorably sliding into organized crime.

Fabrizio wasn't a criminal, far from it. He wasn't interested in money for example. But because the line between 'resistance' and 'terrorism' is sometimes very fine, difficult to feel, I canceled his training overnight and resigned myself to continuing on my own for as long as necessary. The handover wasn't going to happen in the immediate future.

15

"WHY did you stop?"

A series of disturbing incidents led to my decision to step aside.

It all started one July day in 1971. Mattéi had come into the area for color and technical photography in the Rue des Jeûneurs then sat patiently in the waiting room, stroking his mustache as usual. Mattéi was a regular client; by then we'd been working together for eight years. The ritual was that whenever he came to Paris he'd pop in at the laboratory as soon as he arrived, then just before he left. The rest of his time was spent going around the Third World. Disguised as a tourist in a floral shirt and with a camera hanging around his neck, he looked for contacts, arranged secret meetings between the leaders of liberation movements, organized escapes, set up support networks, always with one foot on the ground, the other on the next plane, in all the places where races and nations were fighting for emancipation.

We both had our little habits. His 'package' was always ready, waiting for him in one of the hundreds of boxes of photographic paper stacked against the walls of the darkroom. The 'Mattéi' box, identical to all the others, was the eighth from the bottom in the third stack on the left.

I went to fetch him and took him into the darkroom, taking care to lock the door behind us.

Aways concerned that walls can have ears, inquisitive ears, I'd set up a little radio so we could talk without fear of being overheard and, although M. Petit had already left, we only made small talk until our voices were masked by the music. It was doubtless that my decades working in the underground had made this a reflex action.

Mattéi had come to collect some South African 'internal' passports for the ANC, the African National Congress, the South African anti-apartheid political party. These documents, indispensable for the Black community in South Africa, consisted of an identity card and a police pass. Looked on as foreigners in their own country by the application of the apartheid laws, the Blacks had been expelled from the cities and territories of the Whites to be herded together in reservations—the townships. These documents were essential to allow them to move freely.

Since the ANC's peaceful demonstration in 1960, the organization, judged to be subversive and dangerous, had been outlawed, and its leaders had gone underground. When arrested, the members of the ANC were invariably given life imprisonment; for example, Nelson Mandela, whose imprisonment starting in 1963 moved public opinion worldwide.

It was in that year of 1963 that Mattéi first asked for internal passports; after that the stream of requests was never-ending.

We went over his current needs. Mattéi gave me lists of names and photos, and requested that new Venezuelan and Dominican passports be ready for his next visit.

Then he informed me of a new request. He wanted to know how long it would take to start producing South African 'external' passports. This time it was to allow a large number of anti-apartheid militants to join the ANC leaders in exile and continue the struggle from outside.

I'd never had to make external passports. Mattéi gave me one to serve as a model, doubtless borrowed or stolen, and I set to work a soon as he left.

I examined the original with a magnifying glass. It belonged to a black South African of around thirty who was staring, unsmiling, straight at me from the photo. There was a stamp overlapping the corner of the photo, and the ink had dribbled across the man's shoulder. The passport must have been kept in a trouser pocket. It had a slight coating of grease and was more dog-eared on the right than on the left. The cover was very simply made from solid boards, light brown, with a watermark impressed on it in a slightly darker tint with an emblem above it, die-stamped. It was glued to the pages, of which there were ten or so. I established the format and the weight of the paper, studied its grammage and texture as well as the color, which came in different shades of sepia. The internal pages had impressed watermarks and ruled lines incorporated into the paper. I analyzed the ink used in printing, in the handwriting and in the stamps, and measured the size of the perforations punched in the numbers in order to choose the right needles.

There was no relief stamp and, at first sight, no traps nor any particular difficulties.

I photographed the model page by page, took shots of each stamp and the revenue stamp so that I could photoengrave them, chose my sheets and colored them, incorporated the watermarks, printed them out, made the cover of boards and glued it together.

It took me a week to get the blank prototype passport exactly identical.

I met Mattéi in the *Closerie des lilas*, gave him back the passport I'd used as a model and told him I was just waiting for him to give me the green light.

"We'll see about that when I get back from the Dominican Republic, I'll have the names and photos," he said as he left.

A week later Mattéi still wasn't back from his trip, and I had a phone call from Roland Dumas, who wanted to see me as soon as possible. I went to his place, where I was introduced to Michel Raptis, known as 'Pablo'. Introductions over, Roland left us alone together in a parlor in his office suite.

Although our paths had never crossed, I'd heard a lot about Pablo. In his sixties and of Greek origin, he'd set up a section of the 4th International in Greece before becoming the leader of the Trotskyist party in France. Like me during the war in Algeria, he'd given support to the FLN, notably by being in charge of a gun factory in Morocco. He was also the one who had devised the forged money fiasco in the Netherlands. That operation had failed and led to his arrest as well as that of his accomplices. He'd been sent to prison for fifteen months.

Pablo was reputed to be taking part in most of the struggles for emancipation. Indeed, such was his reputation that when Roland Dumas and Stéphanie had come to ask me to help the Greeks in their fight against the colonels, I'd assumed that their network depended on the Pablists, without, however, being sure.

The only thing was that, however interesting and committed he was, Pablo was the type of person I made it a rule to avoid at all cost. 'Leaky as a sieve' as the underground jargon had it. Too well known to the police forces. Too much of a blabbermouth as well. For me he didn't respect the first law of illegality: when you're working underground you have to observe a certain restraint and thus keep out of the public eye and official political platforms. A question of security and good sense.

Pablo asked me what I'd been doing since I'd supported the FLN.

"Photography. I've specialized in the reproduction of works of art. I have a small firm."

"No forged papers?"

"No."

We exchanged our political opinions, which were markedly similar. We shared the same human values, but I preferred to keep my distance and to remain as evasive as possible about my activities.

After we'd chatted for half an hour, Pablo asked me if I'd be capable of making forged passports. He had one to show me as a model, a South African passport that he held out to me.

Without saying anything I took it to examine it, opened it and was horrified to see that it was the passport I'd given back to Mattéi a week ago. Same photo, same name, same number, same dog-eared corners. I knew this passport by heart—I'd examined it in detail, photographed it, weighed it, gone over it millimeter by millimeter.

"How long would it take you to make some, a hundred, say? Two hundred? Three hundred?"

"I don't know."

"Name me your price. I assure you it'll be mine as well."

I was shocked that he should mention money to me. Was someone taking me for a mercenary again? Anyone who knew me, even if only a little, knew that I categorically refused to accept payment. I'd made working for nothing an absolute principle, for it alone guaranteed my total independence of the networks and kept my commitment incorruptible.

I hid these reflections from Pablo and took the passport with me, telling him I'd let him know later.

Back in my apartment and after a face-to-face with the passport in my kitchen, I had a desperate need to get some sleep. The South African in the photo was looking me up and down, impassive. I'd always made it clear that I insisted on having a sole contact. I'd chosen Mattéi because he was the only one whom I trusted absolutely. He showed strict respect for my system of watertight compartments and had proved a thousand times over that there was no doubt about his intentions. He didn't mention his underground activities to anyone, never took an unnecessary risk. And it wasn't mere chance that as a pair we'd kept going for so many years without obstruction. His complete independence made him different from the others, selecting very carefully the people for whom and with whom he worked.

That Pablo should feel it was his mission to help the ANC, that he should have a need to *be* someone and, above all, to regain his prestige as a militant internationalist that had been seriously compromised by the unfortunate outcome in the Netherlands, didn't surprise me at all.

What I couldn't understand was how the passport had gotten from Mattéi to him and why it should end up with me again. Mattéi wouldn't have given it to Pablo himself because he would have foreseen the risks we would run into working with a person on whom the police had files. And then we'd already sorted out together all the technical elements in producing the passport. Was it Curiel? And in that case, why should he look for another forger, since Mattéi worked for Curiel?

If something serious had happened to Mattéi, I thought, I would have been informed by someone in the network or through the press. Curiel would have found a way of contacting me directly, without going through Pablo. And above all, I was sure Curiel would never have offered me money.

It was impossible to clear my mind of all the questions jostling each other inside my head, making it more and more difficult to get to sleep. What was there behind this business? Two possibilities: either the Curiel network was the source of this shambles, and in that case it unfortunately meant that I was dealing with amateurs totally unaware of the dangers; or we had been infiltrated and somewhere in the group there was a police agent pulling the strings with the aim of breaking up the organization.

The next day I took the passport back to Roland Dumas' place, in an envelope addressed to Pablo, informing him that I didn't intend to follow up his request.

August was approaching and still Mattéi hadn't come to see me. I was getting a little worried and went through the paper from end to end every morning, hoping I wouldn't find his name or his description under news in brief or, worse still, obituaries.

The same as every summer, I shut my firm down for a few weeks. Omar Boudaoud had invited me to go and see him in Algeria. Évelyne had been a partner for me after Lia left. We'd now separated but were still good friends. She wanted to go to Africa, and one day I suggested she accompany me on a vacation in Algeria if, that is, she thought North Africa was sufficiently African. She agreed, so we went on what we called our "breakup trip."

The last time I'd been in Algeria was before the war there, in 1953. I'd never set foot on the soil of independent Algeria.

Some former members of the Jeanson network had settled there, helping to reconstruct the country. They were called 'redfeet'. One of them was Jean-Marie Boeglin.

A journalist at first, then the general secretary of the Théâtre de la Cité in Lyons, he'd joined the FLN support network in the same year as me, 1957. Two years later he'd become the organizer of the network in the Lyons area before he was informed on by a traitor based in Marseilles who, as we later learned, was responsible for the breaking up of the Jeanson network. The day the police came to question him at the theater, he just had time to escape via an emergency exit behind the stage and get to Switzerland. Then to Algeria. Sentenced in his absence to ten years in prison during the Jeanson trial in 1961, he'd never returned to France. In Algiers he became director of the Department of Communications and Environment of the Société nationale de sidérurgie (SNS).[1] We'd never met, but all the good things I'd heard about him and our long telephone conversations had been enough to create an unequivocal sense of brotherhood between us. We couldn't wait to meet.

As soon as I arrived, Boeglin invited me to dinner, and it was as if we'd known each other forever. A simple, warm-hearted get-together. Boeglin was intelligent, welcoming, sincere and above all humane, in every aspect similar to the idea I had of him. The next day I was again invited to dine with him, and the day after and so on for the whole of my stay.

During a never-ending meal, in the course of which we got into high spirits solving the problems of the world, he asked me how I felt about giving a two-week course on photographic technique as a guest lecturer at the Algiers College of Art. As a person who'd always enjoyed training young people, I accepted with pleasure. It was agreed that the course would take place some time after September.

My vacation was about to end, and I went to see Boeglin one last time to say goodbye before I left.

"Joesph, before you go there's something I have to show you."

1. National Iron and Steel Corporation. [MM]

He ushered me into his bedroom, took out the key to his drawer and opened it carefully. "I've been contacted by members of the ANC. They need forged passports so they can get their comrades out of the country. Here's one that can serve as a model."

I had an uneasy feeling as he handed me a South African passport with more pronounced rubbed corners on the right than on the left. I opened it...

It was the same one.

A shiver ran through me. I took a step back and handed him the passport as if it was burning my fingers.

"We'll see about that when I come back," I hastily replied before jumping into a taxi. That all the networks of solidarity with the emancipation of the countries of Africa—and there were lots of them—should need South African passports, fair enough. Nothing more normal. But why always the same passport, three times, in the hands of three different people who didn't mix and didn't even live in the same country? And by what incomprehensible piece of magnetic attraction did it always end up with me? What conclusions should I draw from all that?

Already during the preceding months I'd several times had visits from people I didn't know who introduced themselves as coming from former friends in the FLN support network and who wanted to order documents from me. One after the other I'd politely shown them out. And then there was that dishonest guy, a former member of the FLN support network in Italy, whom I agreed to train for several months until I'd finally lost my temper when, after I'd taught him everything about documents, he asked, "And now money, how d'you make that?"

Yet I'd always done everything to remain invisible, kept out of the light, used pseudonyms and avoided political meetings. I'd never exhibited my pictures, never accepted a medal. But I had to face facts: my name had gotten around too much—now I was in danger.

A young couple were kissing, sitting on the little steps more or less opposite the Roman ruins of the Arènes de Lutèce in Rue Monge, where it joins Rue Rollin. I almost had to step over them to get past and go into the old apartment block with the creaking door and climb the stairs up to the fifth floor.

A lady with the air of an elementary school teacher, presumably his wife, let me in to a dark, modest apartment, the walls covered in books.

"Come in, come in," she said, showing me down a corridor. She indicated a door leading into a little office that was as dark as the rest of the apartment.

Henri Curiel greeted me: "At last I can put a face to the name of 'M. Joseph'!" he exclaimed. "It's more than an honor to meet in flesh and blood the most discreet of behind-the-scenes operators."

He was tall and thin. His stoop, his near-sighted eyes, made tiny by the effect of his thick lenses, his fragile look and his professorial tone had not surprisingly earned him the nickname of the 'Old Man'.

"How long have we been working together without ever having met?" he went on. "In 1959, wasn't it? Twelve years... and the work we've done for our oppressed brothers. To what do I owe the honor of your visit?"

"The same passport three times."

He observed me with a questioning look on his face as I put my large suitcase down on the table before opening it.

"All of this is for you. My stamps, all my pages of calculations and formulas for coloring, blank documents, the models for each document, a machine for heating plastic-coated covers. Look after it all. And I've more stuff for you. When can I bring it around?" Curiel slumped into his armchair without bothering to conceal his annoyance.

It was on the plane coming home from France that I'd made the decision to retire, convinced that if I waited for the solution to the enigma of that damn passport, it was in prison that I'd find it. And locked away in a cell, I'd be no use to anyone.

Boeglin had mentioned a two-year post available in his department of the SNS. At first I'd said no. Then, when he handed me the passport, I thought, "Why not." But just for one year.

My cover had been blown; there was no other word for it. All I could do now was to vanish into thin air, at least for long enough for the intelligence services to forget me. And then I'd done the math. At forty-six I'd been a forger since I was seventeen. Almost thirty years. Surviving that long was something of a miracle in itself.

I knew that my disappearance would be a blow for the Old Man's organization, which was why, when we met, I agreed to take on the training of two apprentice forgers that Mattéi could call on after my forced retirement. As for the anti-Franco Spaniards, I'd already trained enough young forgers for them to be able to manage in the meantime.

My children were grown up, and now they could come and see me as often as they liked. I was single. I owned nothing. All I had to do was to terminate the lease of my apartment and put my firm on ice. M. Petit had done that before when I'd had to flee to Belgium; he'd see to it again.

At the end of December I flew to Algiers with the intention of returning to my life as a forger in a year's time. But I never made any more forged documents, and I spent ten years in Algeria, where I met a young Algerian woman, a law student who had volunteered as an activist for the Movement for the Liberation of Angola (MPLA). That was Leïla, your mother. This time I wanted to make a new start, to live in the open, far from the shadows and the torments of clandestine struggles.

Even today I sometimes think back to my first forged document, when I was seventeen years old. Could I have imagined then that that act was going to mark my life forever? At that time it was the Resistance. For many, that ended with the Liberation. Not for me. My life as a forger is one long, uninterrupted resistance for, after the Nazis, I continued to resist inequality, segregation, racism, injustice, fascism and dictatorships.

I know that there are many people who can't understand my commitment to causes after the end of the Second World War. Since I wasn't in danger anymore, why continue to take the risk of being put in prison or assassinated for such far-away conflicts?

But my involvement in all these struggles was just the logical continuation of what I'd done during the Resistance. In 1944 I saw that freedom could be gained by the determination and courage of a handful of people. As long as it didn't go against honor and human values, a clandestine struggle was a serious, effective means and worthy of consideration.

For thirty years, in my own way and with the only weapons at my disposal—technical knowledge, ingenuity and unshakable utopian ideals—I had fought against a reality that was too harrowing to observe or suffer without doing anything about it. Thanks to my conviction that I had the power to alter the course of things, that there was a better world to be made and that I could make a contribution. A world in which no one would need a forger. It's still my dream.

Epilogue

IN DECIDING TO WRITE about my father's life I deliberately chose to focus on his years of combat alone and to end the narrative in 1971, when he gave up all clandestine political activities. I thought that his other life, the one of which I was part, would only be of interest to his family and close friends. However, when I wrote THE END, there were still some questions left open. Of course I knew his reasons for giving up, but what had happened afterward?

I decided to ask him some more questions.

I arrived in Algiers a few days after the beginning of 1972. A new year, a new life, a new departure. I taught photographic techniques, photoengraving and printing to specially selected students from among the most talented ones at the Algiers College of Art.

I was supposed to be going back to Paris at the start of 1973, but a year passes quickly... I felt fine. I hung around a bit. Then there came the day when a friend in the MLPA asked me to go by car to pick up an activist called Leïla, your mother. A black-skinned woman from the south of Algeria, daughter of a progressive imam, she was extremely beautiful and, I have to say, had many admirers. She was very cultured, was studying law at the University of Algiers, campaigned for the decolonization of Africa and was very interested in contemporary art and photography. It's art that brought us together.

The desire to appeal to her spurred me to imagine a different future. Suddenly, when I'd never thought of it before, I was itching to start everything afresh. I was aware that I'd been incredibly fortunate to escape going to prison, being killed. I drew up a balance sheet. After all, had I not spent enough time as a clandestine, hidden, behind-the-scenes operator giving others life and liberty, without ever concerning myself with my own?

We got married. Your brother Atahualpa was born, then José, then you—it was as if, at the age of fifty—I'd been given a bonus life.

"But then why come back to France ten years later?"

That was Leïla's choice. She sensed that the wave of religious fundamentalism wasn't going to be short-lived. I didn't see anything coming, but she did. As the days passed she noticed how attitudes were getting stricter. She was afraid for you three, 'our little half-castes', she was afraid for me, 'the Jew', and for herself, a liberated woman who'd married me. We had hope that our mixture would be your wealth; now it was putting you in danger. After a hurried departure, we landed in France in 1982 with no baggage, no work, but three young children, a three-month tourist visa and the hope that things would sort themselves out quickly: foreigners, applicants for immigration, concerned that we might all be sent back to our country of origin, though we didn't know exactly where that would be since Leïla was Algerian, you three and me...Argentine. When I came back, I saw Georges

200

Mattéi in *La Clos des lilas* again, just like old times. He'd continued fighting until 1980 and was still working as a journalist and maker of documentaries.

Henri Curiel had died in 1978, assassinated by La Main rouge[1] at the foot of his elevator in Rue Rollin. I'd heard about it in Algeria, from the newspapers. We were both much saddened by Henri's death, which put the seal on the end of an era. We'd grown old—we were no longer in the know. The geopolitical conflicts of the '80s were beyond us; we had no idea what was at stake anymore. I took up my work as a photographer again and applied for naturalization. You have to be able to live in a country where you'll be free. We became French in 1992. I was sixty-seven, and I was a young father! I watched you all grow up hoping that, even if I hadn't been able to give you a better world, I could transmit to you the values for which I've never ceased to fight. Today I'm sure I have.

1. 'The Red Hand', an obscure organization that is assumed to be in reality an offshoot of the French secret service, which they use to get rid of files that are a nuisance by sabotage and assassination. The death of Henri Curiel is generally attributed to the Main rouge or the OAS, though it's not absolutely certain.

Photographs by Adolfo Kaminsky

SELECTION

Stamps, identity cards and passports forged
by Adolfo Kaminsky during the Nazi
occupation of France, including his own
identity card with fingerprint.
The name on this document is
"Julien Keller", lower right.

PHOTO © ADOLFO KAMINSKY

Les enfants
Jeux de bille
1955

PHOTO © ADOLFO KAMINSKY

205

Les puces
Mannequins et manège
1955

PHOTO © ADOLFO KAMINSKY

207

Paris la nuit
Amoureux sur un banc
1948

PHOTO © ADOLFO KAMINSKY

209

Paris la nuit
Femme seule qui attend (Martha Marton)
1946

PHOTO © ADOLFO KAMINSKY

Paris la nuit
Le banc*
1948

*Adolfo Kaminsky often photographed the same scenes,
sometimes quite close to home, in his study of the changing city.

PHOTO © ADOLFO KAMINSKY

213

Paris la nuit
Les Champs Elysées
1952

PHOTO © ADOLFO KAMINSKY

215

Paris la nuit
Vitrines de Pigalle
1952

PHOTO © ADOLFO KAMINSKY

Paris
Le bus
1955

PHOTO © ADOLFO KAMINSKY

Paris
Le libraire
1948

221

Paris
Les enfants
1950

223

Paris
Les pavés
1947

PHOTO © ADOLFO KAMINSKY

225

Paris
Petite fille à la poupée rue Broca
1945

227

Paris
Tunnel sur la Seine
1953

Acknowledgments

For having been kind enough to share their memories with me, I would like to thank Denis Berger, Omar Boudaoud, Marie-Aline Collenot, Hélène Cuenat, maître Roland Dumas, Anita Fernandez, maître Ali Haroun, José Hipolito Dos Santos, Francis Jeanson, Leïla Kaminsky, Marthe Kaminsky, Paul Kaminsky, Marceline Loridan, Yoram Mouchenik, Niko, Sarah-Elisabeth Penn, Belkacem Rhani, Aurélie Ricard, Annette Roger, Suzie Rosenberger, Paul-Louis Thirard and Jean-Pierre Van-Tinguem.

And for reading the manuscript I would like to thank Jean-Étienne Cohen-Séat, Alban Fischer, Nicole Gex, and Leïla Kaminsky.

Biographies

SARAH KAMINSKY is an actress, screenwriter and author born in Algeria. She was three years old when she immigrated to France with her father Adolfo Kaminsky, two brothers and her mother Leïla, a Tuareg Algerian, law student, and anti-colonial activist whose father was a progressive imam. Sarah Kaminsky's first book is the best-selling biography of her father, published by Éditions Calmann-Lévy in 2009 and now translated into seven languages. She has a son and lives in Paris.

ADOLFO KAMINSKY, of Russian Jewish origins and carrying an Argentinean passport, made his living in Paris as a photographer in various fields: postcards, advertising photos, and photo reportage while, at the same time, working clandestinely as an unpaid forger for humanitarian causes. He photographed numerous works of art for exhibition catalogs and posters, and he was the regular documentarian for French painters who were precursors of kinetic art. As a specialist for giant-format photography Adolfo Kaminsky produced film sets for Alexandre Trauner, the set designer for Marcel Carné, René Clair and others. He also took thousands of artistic photographs throughout his life, but has only recently started exhibiting them. He lives in Paris with his wife, Leïla.

MIKE MITCHELL has been active as a translator for over thirty years. He is the recipient of the Schlegel-Tieck Prize for translations of German works published in Britain, has won the British Comparative Literature Association translation competition twice for works from German along with a commendation for a translation from French, and has been short-listed for numerous other awards. In 2012 the Austrian Ministry of Education, Art and Culture awarded him a lifetime achievement award as a translator of literary works. He lives in Scotland.